IS GOD A WHITE RACIST?

William R. Jones is a Unitarian-Universalist minister and a professor at the Yale Divinity School. He received his Ph.D. from Brown University in 1968 and has been published in numerous magazines, including HARVARD THEOLOGICAL REVIEW, CHRISTIAN CENTURY, RELIGIOUS EDUCATION, and REFLECTION.

IS GOD A WHITE RACIST?

A Preamble to Black Theology

by William R. Jones

C. ERIC LINCOLN SERIES ON BLACK RELIGION

ANCHOR BOOKS

ANCHOR PRESS/DOUBLEDAY

GARDEN CITY, NEW YORK

Published simultaneously in hard and paperback editions by Anchor Press/
Doubleday & Company, Inc. in 1973.

Anchor Books edition: 1973

ISBN: 0-385-00995-X

CONTENTS

FOREWORD   vii
ACKNOWLEDGMENTS   ix
PROLOGUE   xi
INTRODUCTION   xiii

PART I.   *An Overview of Divine Racism*
     I.   Divine Racism: A Philosophical and Theo-
          logical Analysis   3
    II.   White God—Black Protest   24
   III.   Should a Priest Call a Doctor? Theodicy,
          Oppression, and Quietism   40
    IV.   Divine Racism and Theological Method   61

PART II. *Black Suffering and Black Theology: An
          Internal Critique*
     V.   Divine   Racism: The   Unacknowledged
          Threshold Issue for Black Theology   71
    VI.   Joseph Washington: Blacks as God's Suf-
          fering Servant   79
   VII.   James Cone: God, Champion of the Op-
          pressed   98
  VIII.   Albert Cleage: God, A Black Soul Brother   121
    IX.   Major Jones: Man, Cosufferer with God   132
     X.   J. Deotis Roberts: A Psychology of Black
          Liberation   145

vi

PART III. *Toward a Black Theodicy for Today*
XI. Toward a Prolegomenon to Black Theology 169
XII. Humanocentric Theism: A Theistic Framework for Ethnic Suffering 185

EPILOGUE 203
NOTES 204
INDEX 233

FOREWORD

This series of books is about the black religious experience. It is addressed to Blackamericans, because the rich heritage that is their history has not been made fully available to them in the usual ways in which a society informs its membership about the significant aspects of its development. Blackamericans want to know—indeed they *must* know—more about who they *were* and who they *are* if they are seriously concerned about who they intend to become. The black man's religion is a critical component of his American passage from slavery to a freedom that is still to be perfected.

This series is addressed to white America too. The black experience—religious, social, economic, political—is writ large in the cultural development of the larger society. Understanding it is crucial to an informed perspective of what America is or can become. To a degree not always recognized, America is what it is because the black minority is here and has been here since long before this nation came into being.

The blacks brought their religion with them. After a time they accepted the white man's religion, but they have not always expressed it in the white man's way. It became the black man's purpose—perhaps it was his *destiny*—to shape, to fashion, to re-create the religion offered him by the Christian slave master, to remold it nearer to his own heart's desire, nearer to his own peculiar needs. The black religious experience is something more than a black patina on a white happening. It is a unique response to a historical occurrence that can never be replicated for any people in America.

The black man's pilgrimage in America was made less onerous because of his religion. His religion was the organizing principle around which his life was structured. His church was his school, his forum, his political arena, his social club, his art gallery, his conservatory of music. It was lyceum and gymnasium as well as sanctum sanctorum. His religion was his fellowship with man, his audience with God. It was the peculiar sustaining force that gave him the strength to endure when endurance gave no promise, and the courage to be creative in the face of his own dehumanization.

This is the black religious experience. This is what this book and this series are about.

C. Eric Lincoln
Union Theological Seminary

ACKNOWLEDGMENTS

I wish to express my gratitude to Professors Eugene Holmes and Winston McAllister, my philosophy mentors at Howard University, and Professors Stephen Crary and Wendell Dietrich, my major thesis advisers at Brown University. I am also indebted to Yale University for several summer grants.

Special thanks must be tendered to the students in my class on Black Theology, where the argument of this book was first launched. Their critical and sympathetic response to my tentative formulations did much to sharpen the final product. I am also deeply indebted to Professor Paul Lehmann of Union Theological Seminary for a careful reading of the first draft of the manuscript. His perceptive criticisms resulted in important improvements in the arrangement and emphases of the final manuscript. Most of all I am grateful to my editor, C. Eric Lincoln, for his limitless patience and encouragement and for steering me away from my worst mistakes. An author publishing for the first time could not ask for a better guide.

Finally, the real sacrifice that made this study possible has been shouldered by my wife, Lauretta, and my two sons, Jeffrey David and Darrell Roger. I can only hope that this effort merits my regrettable absence from their lives as husband and father.

To those whose lives have taught me the meaning of self-sacrificing love:

My wife, Lauretta

My mother, Lannie B. Jones (1900–68)

My father, Henry W. Jones, Jr.

PROLOGUE

Think not, as you read these pages, that they were conceived in certainty and ease. Fear and trembling, confusion and doubt gave them birth. And if my words bespeak an irreverent iconoclasm and profane dissent for the sake of notoriety, they contradict my conscious motives.

One question impelled and animated my search in this book, a question phrased most eloquently by Du Bois decades ago, a question he addressed to God but that I direct to the reader:

O God? How long shall the mounting flood of innocent blood roar in Thine ears and pound in our hearts for vengeance? . . . Forgive us, good Lord, we know not what we say! Bewildered we are and passion-tossed, mad with the madness of a mobbed and mocked and murdered people; straining at the armposts of Thy throne, we raise our shackled hands and charge Thee, God, by the bones of our stolen fathers, by the tears of our dead mothers, by the very blood of Thy crucified Christ: What meaneth this? Tell us the plan; give us the sign![1]

Dear reader, tell me the sign; help me find the plan.

INTRODUCTION

Each of the current black theologians—Albert Cleage, James Cone, Major Jones, J. Deotis Roberts, and Joseph Washington—has answered in his own way Du Bois' perplexing question, What meaneth black suffering? However, their answers, individually and collectively, compound the confusion of an already inscrutable mystery. They have painstakingly drawn a theological road map to guide the black faithful from distorted conceptions to prophetic enlightenment. But the road is full of logical potholes, theological washouts, and elaborate but unsound detours. Consequently the theological terrain they have scouted must be surveyed again.

It has often been said that asking the right question is as important as supplying the correct answer. Whether correct or incorrect, this generalization describes the purpose in the following pages. To paraphrase Kant's admonition, my objective is to force the black theologians and their readers to pause a moment and, neglecting all that they have said and done, to reconsider their conclusions in the light of another question: Is God a white racist? My concern throughout is to illuminate the issues this pregnant question introduces into the arena of black theology and religion. The black theologian, I contend, cannot avoid this issue of divine racism, because it is implicit in his theological method, purpose, and content.

No doubt the combination of terms "divine" and "racism" is novel—some will say blasphemous. But the ideas and categories the concept expresses are time-honored and familiar themes in philosophy and theology. To raise the question of divine racism is actually to revive a perennial issue in black religion: what is the meaning, the cause, and the "why" of black suffering? It is to resurrect for this day and time the same question Du Bois probed a half century ago.

In a more general vein the issue of divine racism is simply another way of addressing the traditional problem of evil and human suffering. "The Problem of Suffering Revisited" is an apt description of a central emphasis of this book. In more technical terms the question "Is God a white racist?" pushes the issue of theodicy[1] to the forefront of theological discussion.

Because the concept of divine racism is novel, it is perhaps best to begin the analysis autobiographically, tracing, as it were, the evolution of the concept in my own mind.

A number of experiences and influences converged to give form and flesh to the concept of divine racism as I have entertained it. First among these is my status as a member of an oppressed minority. To be oppressed, in the final analysis, is to suffer, and to suffer in a way that differs radically from the suffering of those who have not known oppression. Indeed it would be surprising if the oppressed did not reflect upon the nature, the cause, and the justice of their suffering, since suffering prescribes the permanent predicament of the oppressed.

Allied to this general influence is my background in the black church—though I admit that the reader may be hard pressed to detect its traces on these pages. The sermons of my grandfather, Sunday-school lessons on the Exodus, the Cross, the suffering servant, etc., provided my earliest answers to the enigma of black suffering. It will become evident that I have rejected these solutions forged in my childhood, but one must not conclude that to reject what is learned in one's youth is necessarily to be free of its formative influences.

These influences account in large part for my enduring interest in the problem of evil and human suffering. A quick survey of my undergraduate and graduate term papers and of the courses I have taught reveals the problem of evil to be the single and most prominent thread running through the whole skein of my personal and scholarly interests.

There is also a group of thinkers I label "black humanists." I have in mind those few but fearless spokesmen who rejected the biblical and Christian models for explaining black suffering, who were unafraid to doubt God's intrinsic goodness relative to blacks, who questioned God's existence and relevance in the struggle for black freedom.[2] It is characteristic of most writers on black religion to relegate black humanism to a theological limbo. James Cone and Benjamin Mays, for instance, classify it as "secular," "non-religious" and "anti-religious,"[3] thus denying its value and status as an authentic expression of the black religious experience. This interpretation of black humanism must be challenged. Black humanism is antithetical to traditional Western theism, black or white, but we can label it non-religious only if we equate religion and theism. An indirect concern of this study is to compel a rehearing for this aspect of black religious thought. It is also my concern to make this humanistic wing of black religion the norm for contemporary black theology, thereby providing a more realistic interpretation of the meaning of the black experience.

Add to these black humanists the humanism of Albert Camus and Jean-Paul Sartre, the French existentialists. I have benefited from the influence of both, although my own philosophical position is much closer to my understanding of Sartre's humanistic existentialism. My own thinking and my reading of the black humanists, of Camus and Sartre, and of certain others[4] suggest the following concepts, which undergird the central argument of this book: theodicy as the central theological category, the possibility of a demonic God, and the intimate connection between theodicy and oppression. These propositions, coupled with some salient critiques of the principal theodicies in the Christian tradition, inform my critical understanding of the central issues in black theology and black religion.

An obvious place to look for parallels to the black experience in religion is the theological treatment of Jewish oppression, the suffering of another ethnic minority. One work stands out here, Rabbi Richard Rubenstein's *After Auschwitz*.[5] His analysis of Jewish suffering forced me to pose a troublesome question that he does not explicitly consider: Is God an anti-Semite? The implications of his study for my own explorations in black theology were direct and immediate. In the light of black suffering, a suffering that may exceed that of the Jews,[6] the unsettling question becomes: Is God a white racist?

Moreover, Rubenstein, like the black humanists and like Camus and Sartre, pressed certain points of critical import for theological method. The oppression and slaughter of the Jews in World War II convinced him that only one standard should be used to evaluate Jewish theology: its ability to assimilate the horror of Auschwitz, the mass murder of six million Jews. Thus Rubenstein's argument makes the analysis of Jewish suffering the necessary point of departure for the Jewish theologian, and the viability of its theodicy becomes the touchstone for an authentic Jewish theology.

At this juncture of the investigation the inevitable conclusion seemed that the correlative concepts of black suffering and theodicy were the imperative foci for a black theology worthy of acceptance, and my reading of the inner logic of the extant black theologians reaffirmed this conclusion. Subsequent investigations added nothing substantially new to the general position already supported methodologically by Frederick Sontag's analyses in *God, Why Did You Do That?*[7] and *The God of Evil*.[8] Hence the major contours of the concept and its methodological implications were already firmly established.

A further conclusion—and here begins the outline of the

three divisions of this book—is that the issue of divine racism emerges only in particular theological contexts; not every theological framework forces this issue. The first purpose of Part I is to identify the combination of theological categories and frameworks that makes it necessary to ask, Is God a white racist? The issue of divine racism surfaces whenever a specific type of suffering, which I identify as *ethnic suffering,* is joined with particular interpretations of God's sovereignty over human history and His activity within human history or both. Hence the initial exploration of the concept of human suffering from several perspectives, with the intent of establishing divine racism as not only a legitimate but an irreducible theological category.

The description and analysis of the category of divine racism serve as the background for the second purpose of Part I, which is to establish the centrality of theodicy for black theology. Johannes Metz has argued that the demands of Christian faith require "the development of theology as eschatology." He further concludes that eschatology "must not be reduced to a *part* of Christian theology but must be understood radically: as the determining factor in all theological statements."[9] I maintain that black theology demands a different arrangement of the theological furniture. For it, theodicy must assume the first rank, which Metz assigns to eschatology.

A former colleague responded to my claim about the centrality of theodicy with this criticism: My concern to make theodicy the essential nucleus of black theology is illegitimate, for it means that I am forcing the formal question of theodicy. That is to say, I am comprehending black theology in the tradition of Western religious philosophy and its conventional problems. In sum, he concluded, I do not sufficiently honor the black perspective.

This is an eminently fair challenge, and the bulk of this book is an implicit reply to it. I would argue that I am not elevating theodicy to a rank it does not already enjoy in black theology and theology in general. Theodicy, I will show, is already at the heart of theology; I simply call attention to this fact.

I conclude that each person has a functional theodicy; there is an aspect of his over-all world view that treats the issue of suffering and relates it to his prevailing beliefs about the nature of ultimate reality and man. It is not difficult, for instance, to demonstrate that each individual makes a fundamental judgment about the character of specific sufferings, whether each is good (positive), bad (negative), or neutral; whether he must endure the suffering he encounters or should annihilate it; whether suffering can be eliminated or whether it is an inevitable part of the human condition. Each person also acts on the basis of some conclusion about the source or cause of suffering. Indeed it would be surprising if mankind as a whole did not ordinarily reflect upon suffering, since it appears to be an inescapable aspect of the human condition.[10]

The universal concern with the issue of suffering and theodicy is often overlooked, and the reason is not hard to isolate. Theodicy, we must first consider, is defined too narrowly. The common understanding of theodicy places too much emphasis upon its etymology; for too many, *theos,* God, and *dikē,* justice, comprise the total meaning. But an etymological analysis illuminates only one aspect of the enterprise of theodicy, namely the apologetic. Theodicy is more than the attempt to exonerate and justify God's purpose and works in the face of contrary evidence. There is another dimension; for instance, a concern to determine the cause of suffering. In fact every apologetic approach to human suffering is at the same time an implicit conclusion about the cause or origin of suffering.

Theodicy is also defined too narrowly if it is perceived as an abstract and theoretical enterprise executed only by professional philosophers and theologians. What is the suffering-servant theme in Isaiah but a theodicy in miniature? Is not Du Bois engaged in the enterprise of theodicy when he asks, "What meaneth this?"

Indeed it does not do violence to the total salvation history of Christian faith—the creation, the fall of man, the incarnation and resurrection of Jesus, the second coming of Jesus—to interpret it as a pattern of theodicy as well as salvation. In fact I would argue that theodicy is the necessary ground for salvation. That is to say, theodicy is logically prior to the affirmation of the salvation of man. To talk about the *saving* work of God is to presuppose a conclusion about the *benevolence* of God; it is to assert the essential goodness of God in spite of the prior "evil" that makes his "saving" work necessary. In sum, salvation is meaningless without the prior affirmation of God's benevolence toward man. The priority of theodicy is further underscored when we consider—and one of the major arguments of this book is to demonstrate the point—that every alleged act of God's benevolence can easily be interpreted as an instance of His malevolence.

Several arguments will establish that theodicy is the controlling category for black theology, and this will be accomplished in a manner that does not involve the use of concepts alien to a black perspective. One argument will show that theodicy is central because black theology defines itself as a theology of liberation. Accordingly, the special requirements of a theology of liberation necessitate consideration of the theodicy issue. This becomes clear if some of the essentials of a theology of liberation are identified by considering some general observations about oppression and suffering.

Oppression, I contend, is reducible to a form of suffering. If one dichotomizes between negative and positive suffering, oppression is a variety of negative suffering. It involves a suffering that is either detrimental or irrelevant to one's highest good. It is also noteworthy that if a positive quality is assigned to suffering, as for instance in masochism, suffering is welcomed and willingly endured. However, to define suffering as negative motivates one to crush it. The theologian of liberation, by definition, is committed to annihilate oppression, which is to say, to eliminate the suffering that is the heart of oppression. Thus he must provide an explanation that perceives the suffering as negative. He must show that the suffering that is oppression is not God's will or sanctioned by nature. He must, in sum, desanctify the suffering in question, or else the oppressed will not regard their suffering as oppressive and will not be motivated to attack it. The theologian or philosopher of liberation, in short, *must* engage in the enterprise of theodicy if he is to accomplish his task.

A second argument for the centrality of theodicy concludes that the unique character of black suffering forces the question of divine racism, and to pose this question is to initiate the theodicy debate. The black theologian is obliged to reconcile the inordinate amount of black suffering, which is implied in his claim that the black situation is oppressive, with his affirmations about the nature of God and God's sovereignty over human history.

Jürgen Moltmann has correctly perceived that today the theodicy question has assumed a new form and also a new importance in theology:

> Since we experience reality as history and no longer as cosmos, the fundamental theodicy question is still with us and is more pressing than before. For us it has no longer only its old naturalistic form, as in the earthquake of Lisbon in 1775. It appears today in a political form, as in the question of Auschwitz. . . . We ask the question: *An Deus sit?* ("Whether God is") on grounds of history and its crimes. . . .[11]

I suggest that, at least for America, it is black suffering, not Auschwitz, that introduces the theodicy question. Accordingly, a viable theodicy, one that refutes the charge of divine racism, must be the point of departure and the necessary foundation for the construction of a black theology. This is not to demand that a theodicy must be a kind of preface to any black theology. Rather, my contention is that the theodicy question must control the entire theological enterprise and be its ultimate foundation. What the black theologian wishes to assert about the person and work of Jesus (Christology) or the ultimate consummation of human destiny (eschatology) must be viewed in terms of its connection to the problem of black suffering. In short the essential conclusion of Part I is that black theology must be an extended theodicy.

Part II of this study critically analyzes the respective positions of the most popular black theologians—Albert Cleage, James Cone, Major Jones, J. Deotis Roberts, and Joseph Washington—on the issue of black suffering. Part I provides the critical apparatus for that analysis. It is possible to read and appreciate Part I without a knowledge of the field of black theology and its literature. Part II, however, one cannot. In a real sense it is a "family squabble" internal to black theology. The present situation in black theology and the peculiar themes of this study mean that throughout, but particularly in Part II, I am engaged, hopefully, in an instructive debate with the best-known black theologians.

Part II aims at several demonstrations: I purport to show that the issue of divine racism is in fact forced by the black theologians' own conclusions and presuppositions. Having adopted specific theological frameworks and concepts, e.g. the politics of God, the question "Is God a white racist?" inexorably surfaces. Moreover, I contend that the scaffolding of their respective systems collapses if they do not refute the charge of divine racism.

Having shown the necessity of a viable theodicy that invalidates the claim of divine racism, I then proceed to analyze critically the respective answers the black theologians give to the mystery of black suffering. The critical test I utilize is whether the black theologian consistently disproves the charge of divine racism and whether his account of black suffering provides a coherent and sturdy foundation for the theology of liberation advanced as its explicit purpose. When this test is applied, I reach the unobscure conclusion that each of the black theologies examined is defective. All leave the issue of divine racism unresolved. In some cases the issue is not even raised for consideration, even though its refutation is presupposed by the essential position taken by the black theologian. The resolution thus begs the question: it takes for granted what must be proved. In other instances the argument is not tenable because of the questionable logical and theological positions it requires for its support.

The conclusions of Parts I and II force an issue that is the focus of Part III. Given the necessity of a viable theodicy (the conclusion of Part I) and given that none of the black theologians provides that indispensable theodicy (the conclusion of Part II), it is necessary to determine what other theodicies can meet the needs of an authentic black theodicy. This is the purpose of Part III.

Though an extensive discussion of classical solutions to the theodicy question falls outside the scope of my present analysis, I feel compelled to state that my research in this area indicates that they are not adequate to account for ethnic suffering. Nor do I find that the solution of John Hick[12] and the theologians of hope fares better than those of the black theologians. Hence my conclusion that a new model for treating black suffering must be sought. I suggest that what I term *humanocentric theism* and *"secular" humanism* are the best candidates. The essential feature of both is the advocacy of the *functional ultimacy of man*. Man must act *as if* he were the ultimate valuator or the ultimate agent in human history or both. Thus God's responsibility for the crimes and errors of human history is reduced if not effectively eliminated.

Of special interest in this respect is the identification of those features of the black theologians that must be modified if humanocentric theism or secular humanism is accepted as normative. The belief, for instance, that blacks are God's chosen people must be abandoned. This section also serves as a brief introduction to my own statement of a theology or philosophy of liberation that is still in its formative stage.

PART I

✣✣✣✣✣✣✣✣✣✣✣✣

An Overview of Divine Racism

DIVINE RACISM:
A PHILOSOPHICAL AND THEOLOGICAL
ANALYSIS

Toward a Definition of Divine Racism

Because of the novelty of the concept of divine racism, it is beneficial to describe its essential features by examining some concrete examples in which the concept is highly visible. Thomas Gossett's interpretation of sections of the *Rig Veda,* the Hindu scriptures of ancient India, and I. A. Newby's analysis of "religious racism"[1] provide the desired specimens.

In Gossett's interpretation, Indra, the God of the Aryans, is described as "blowing away with supernatural might from earth and from the heavens the black skin which Indra hates." The account further reports how Indra "slew the flat-nosed barbarians," the dark people called Anasahs. Finally, after Indra conquers the land of the Anasahs for His worshipers, He commands that the Anasahs are to be "flayed of [their] black skin."[2]

Proposition one. The first distinctive trait of divine racism to be noted is its appeal to a "two-category system";[3] it presupposes a basic division of mankind into an "in" group and an "out" group. In addition, this fundamental division is supported, initiated, or sanctioned by God Himself. God has special concern for the "in" group, and it receives His sustaining aid and grace. By contrast He is indifferent or hostile to the "out" group. In sum, God does not value all men equally; consequently He treats them differently. And this difference is not accidental but central to His will and purpose.

Proposition two. In the context of divine racism, the two-category system is correlated with an imbalance of suffering; the "out" group suffers more than the rest of the population. In the account from the *Rig Veda* we know that God has less affection for the Anasahs, because they suffer far more than the Aryans. The Anasahs are the vanquished, not the victor.

Proposition three. Implicit in the concept of divine racism is a third principle: God is responsible for the imbalance of suffering that differentiates the "in" and the "out" groups. Indra is the major warrior on the field of battle bringing about the Anasahs' defeat. Thus honor, praise, and thanksgiving are addressed to Him for His mighty acts in slaying "the flat-nosed barbarians." Perhaps, however, the concept of divine racism is defined too narrowly if it must be God's own hand that flays the ethnic outcasts. For my purpose I would emphasize only that the imbalance of suffering must express God's will or purpose, thus allowing that men or angels, for instance, could be the actual instrument and executioners of the divine plan.

Proposition four. God's favor or disfavor is correlated with the racial or ethnic identity of the group in question. God's wrath and hostility are directed toward the very features that characterize a particular racial or ethnic community. As the account from the *Rig Veda* concludes, Indra hated their blackness.

Proposition five. Newby's analysis of religious racism—"the idea that racial inequality is the work and will of God"—[4] describes another essential feature of divine racism: God must be a member of the "in" group. In the context of this study, God must be white. The argument of an American divine, the Reverend Buchner Payne, is a classic statement of this claim:

Now as Adam was white, Abraham white and our Savior white, did he enter heaven when he arose from the dead as a white man or as a negro? If as a white man, then the negro is left out; if as a negro then the white man is left out. As Adam was the Son of God and as God is light (white) and in Him is no darkness (black) at all, how could God then be the father of the negro, as like begets like? And if God could not be the father of the blacks because He was white, how could our Savior, "being the express image of God's person," as asserted by St. Paul, carry such a damned color into heaven, where all are white, much less to the throne?[5]

Clearly Payne's analysis presupposes the two-category system, here the saved and the unsaved. This difference is correlated with contrasting racial populations, black and white. Salvation, the highest expression of God's favor, occurs only when the savior and the elect belong to the same ethnic group.

It is necessary at this juncture, for the sake of accuracy, to make certain qualifications. It must be understood that I am not arguing that every concept of divine election or divine preference is divine racism. We must allow that God may select a special group or individual to accomplish the salvation of others. But this type of election is more a specification of function, and need not entail in any way that God's love is less than universal.

Nor should one conclude that God's direct or indirect flaying or even the slaughter of a particular group is sufficient evidence for divine racism. The possibility that flaying is a justified response to prior sin must be granted. It is illegitimate to allow the concept of divine punishment to collapse into a form of divine racism.[6]

Having identified and qualified some of the prominent features of divine racism, it is now necessary to scrutinize each. We must determine if every one of the several traits is essential and what special problems arise when we try to ascertain if divine racism is in fact present. Consider, for instance, that the fourth and fifth propositions introduce unique problems. The fourth requires ultimately that we psychoanalyze God, that we read His mind and fathom His motive and intent, His value system and plan for mankind. The fifth necessitates that the very being of God must be visible to the human observer. The third proposition involves a similar difficulty: We must either identify where God's own hand is at work in human history or at least specify the human acts that are claimed to be the locus of His activity. Merely to state the problem is to illuminate the difficulty. Some question from another perspective must also be raised regarding the fourth proposition. Is blackness really the object of white hatred and racism? I think not. The racist is not actually affirming that white skin color is superior to black skin color. His emphasis lies elsewhere. The alleged inferiority and undesirability of blacks, which lie at the core of racism, do not inhere in color; it is of a different order, e.g. intelligence. Blackness is simply the most visible indicator of the absence or presence of the latter.

If we doubt the possibility of psychoanalyzing God to determine the presence of divine racism, if the divine side of the coin is obscure, then attention must be directed to the human side. This dictates that we plumb the situation of man, especially the factor of suffering and its uneven distribution. Thus my approach to the issue of divine racism reduces primarily to an analysis of the second proposition, to which we now turn.

The Multievidentiality of Suffering

To speak of divine racism is to raise questions about God's equal love and concern for all men. It is to suggest that He is for some but not for others, or at least not for all equally. It asks whether there is a demonic streak in the divine nature. The charge of divine racism, in the final analysis, is a frontal challenge to the claim of God's benevolence for all.

No doubt the phrase "divine racism" falls on the ear with

contradictory import; it is akin to speaking of a married bachelor or a square circle. This is so, precisely because the concept of God's benevolence is being attacked. The case is the same with any God talk that hints at a demonic God. Only by picturing God as a supernatural Dr. Jekyll and Mr. Hyde can space be found for a malevolent deity. Clearly, in the context of Western monotheism, benevolence is as essential to the definition of God as is His existence. Hence there is an instinctive tendency to make God and goodness interchangeable terms and an inclination to make either man or some other creature, e.g. the devil, the ultimate cause of evil. One point is unmistakable in the framework of the Judaeo-Christian tradition: we can establish the legitimacy and irreducibility of the category of divine racism only by a frontal attack on the concept of God's *intrinsic* goodness.

The quickest and most effective way to execute this attack is to show that events are multievidential; specifically, the materials and events that have traditionally been interpreted as evidence of divine benevolence can just as easily support the opposite conclusion, of divine malevolence. Albert Camus makes this point persuasively in his inverted interpretation of Jesus' crucifixion, when he argues that the Cross is not necessarily a sign of God's activity for man's salvation.

Golgotha, a symbol of Jesus' suffering, traditionally represents God's crowning act of self-sacrificing love and vicarious suffering for man's salvation. And if we emphasize Anders Nygren's[7] view, Calvary expresses the very essence of agapaic love, with no hint of divine self-interest.

Camus's interpretation of the inner meaning of Golgotha, however, has a strong flavor of misanthropy and divine self-interest:

For as long as the Western world has been Christian, the Gospels have been the interpreter between heaven and earth. Each time a solitary cry of rebellion against human suffering was uttered, the answer came in the form of an even more terrible suffering. In that Christ had suffered

and had suffered voluntarily, suffering was no longer unjust. . . . From this point of view the New Testament
can be considered as an attempt to answer, in advance,
every [rebel] by painting the figure of God in softer colors
and by creating an intercessor between God and man.
Christ came to solve two major problems, evil and death.
. . . His solution consisted first in experiencing them. The
man-god suffers, too—with patience. Evil and death can
no longer be entirely imputed to Him, since He, too, suffers and dies.[8]

The effect of Camus's interpretation is to deny that Calvary is
linked to man's salvation. In this new setting it becomes a public relations gimmick concocted by God to improve His image
by reducing His accountability for human suffering. By arguing that human suffering should be endured and accepted
because God Himself has suffered even more, the strategy is
laid to keep man, particularly the oppressed, docile and reconciled to his suffering. Accordingly, human suffering does not
become a springboard to rebellion. The one act that will initiate man's ultimate deliverance and humanization, the one act
that will dignify man is nipped in the bud—precluded, as it
were, by God's supreme act of love! God's act in Christ, then,
becomes not an act for man's highest good, but against it.
And the principle that we should love God because He first
loved us collapses.

The essential focus of Camus's argument is to call attention
to the ambiguity or multievidentiality of events. This means
that the same event points with equal validity toward opposing interpretations. Multievidentiality is especially prominent
when we are dealing with an individual's motive. Whether we
conclude that God is a liberator or a misanthrope on the
grounds of Calvary rests finally upon our reading of His motive. The multievidentiality of phenomena is also pronounced
when we consider a general situation rather than a single event.
It is interesting to compare how different observers describe the
black situation in America. The black theologians, particularly

James Cone, Joseph Washington, and J. Deotis Roberts, discover the liberating hand of God at work in the present black
condition. Samuel Yette, however, sees a different pattern: "a
plan to 'destroy' an obsolete people."[9] Liberation or genocide?
Take your pick.

The crucial conclusion, therefore, to be drawn from Camus's
analysis is this: a demonic deity is a possible deduction—I do
not say the only one—from every event asserting God's benevolence. And the step is indeed a short one from a demonic
deity to a divine racist.

The divine suffering at Golgotha yields a possible interpretation of divine hostility. A similar conclusion can be drawn
from any instance of human suffering; it, too, is multievidential. Any given occurrence of human suffering harmonizes
equally well with antithetical positions, divine favor or disfavor,
God's grace or God's curse.[10] Consequently, in the face of human suffering, whatever its character, we must entertain the
possibility that it is an expression of divine hostility. Moreover,
if it is allowed that the general category of human suffering
raises the possibility of a demonic deity, then the particular
category of black suffering—and this is the crucial point for
the argument—at least suggests the possibility of divine racism,
a particular form of hostility.

A critical question arises once we acknowledge that suffering is multievidential: can we determine which of the antithetical interpretations is correct by inspecting the suffering itself?
As a general principle, I would answer "No." Though black
suffering may raise the question of divine racism or malevolence, the answer cannot be determined by an examination of
that suffering alone. Camus's analysis of Golgotha illustrates
the point. His interpretation of a demonic deity is not based
on any peculiarities of suffering; no special aspects of Calvary
demand an interpretation of divine hostility. Rather, Camus
brings a different theological perspective to his analysis of the
materials. The decisive factor appears to be his refusal to presuppose the intrinsic goodness of God because he adopts a different interpretive principle: God is the sum of his acts.

God as the Sum of His Acts

The concept of divine racism becomes clearer when we connect the previous discussion, of the multievidentiality of suffering and a demonic deity, to the principle: man is the sum of his acts. This principle is central to Sartre's doctrine of man, but I will argue subsequently that it is also central to the biblical understanding of God.

When we unpack the essentials of the principle that man is the sum of his acts, we find the following to be crucial for the discussion. First, a man's *character* is the sum of his acts. To speak of a man as loving or honest is always to refer to a complex of loving *acts,* of honest acts. The principle thus places what amounts to exclusive weight on the individual's activity, and this involves a corresponding devaluation of the category of motives. Indeed, in the context of this principle, a motive is an inference from the real acts of the individual. To assign a motive commits one to a particular method of confirmation. A motive must be substantiated—and this is the crucial point for the analysis—by reference to the actual practice of the individual. That is to say, we verify motives, as it were, retrospectively. We look at the individual's actual behavior and then argue backward to a prior motive. Thus the consequence of this principle is clear; we cannot appeal to an alleged self or character that is independent of or in disharmony with the veritable acts of the person.

The principle that man is the sum of his acts also places a premium upon the present and past acts of an individual. The character or motive we assign must be substantiated by reference to one's actual actions, i.e. past and/or present. Appeal cannot be made to one's anticipated or future acts as determinative for an appraisal of one's present character.

This point takes on additional clarity when we consider a third consequence of the principle. To speak of man as the sum of his acts is to advance a specific theory about man's nature, namely that man is freedom. Freedom, in this context, is the essence of man, and it alone is intrinsic. Accordingly we must differentiate between the *given* essence of man and his *achieved* essence. The former designates man's freedom; the latter, the character he weaves through the exercise of his given essence, i.e. freedom. More specifically, love, honesty, etc. must be classified as aspects of one's achieved essence and therefore are never intrinsic. Love, like the other aspects of one's achieved essence, refers, then, to one's actual perform-ance, the sum of one's acts.

Applying the principle that man is the sum of his acts to God, we arrive at some illuminating conclusions, particularly for theological method and treatments of suffering that appeal to a future, or eschatological, resolution. First, it requires that whatever motive or character is assigned to God must be based on His past or present acts or both. Further, one is not per-mitted to speak of a divine motive of character that is dif-ferent from His actual performance relative to man.

This principle obviously presents apparently insurmountable difficulties for the black theologian, for it forces him to identify the actual events in which he sees the benevolent and liberating hand of God at work not for man in general, but for blacks. This is not easily accomplished in light of the long history of oppression that is presupposed by each black theologian.

Treatments of suffering that appeal to eschatological, i.e. future, data are also seriously threatened if not effectively demolished by the principle that God is the sum of His acts. The reasons for this conclusion are simple. Every eschatologi-cal theory presupposes that man's situation in the future will differ from his past or present condition. According to this theory the shape and character of human existence will be radically modified; the Christian hope is that the undesirable elements of the past and the present will be judiciously elimi-nated or transformed. Many biblical images come to mind to confirm this observation. "The wolf shall dwell with the lamb."[11] "The blind receive their sight, the lame walk, . . . the dead are raised up."[12] The eschatological approach looks toward a corrective development in the course of human history. Whether the future is interpreted to involve a more complete realization of something already in germ or whether the future is said to involve a radical and qualitative break with present conditions, the corrective element is still clearly visible. And it is the corrective factor that is significant for the subsequent argument.

That many black theologians quickly accept an eschatological approach to black suffering is surprising in light of the troublesome consequences that attend its adoption. Does this acceptance suggest a certain desperation of method or argument? We can get at one weighty problem by asking the question, Why has the anticipated amelioration of black suffering not yet occurred; why is there still a double portion of black suffering? Surely the delay of the new age of black freedom yields at least these two interpretations: (1) being able but not wanting to; (2) wanting to but being unable. And these alternatives correspond roughly to the respective theories of a malevolent and a benevolent deity.

A further point is worthy of consideration: Consider that the anticipated correction can be read as either a gratuitous hope or a question-begging device—if it is not substantiated in a precise way. On what grounds can the black theologian affirm that God's activity will be different in the future—i.e., effecting the liberation of blacks—when the present and past history of blacks is oppression? Must not the evil and suffering that are presupposed in the very hope for future improvement be regarded as possible counterevidence against two claims: that the future will be different and that God will act differently in the future, i.e. in a liberating fashion? And as possible contrary evidence, must it not be considered and refuted by those who adopt the opposite interpretation?

Black religionists appear to beg the question in their appeal to the future. Believing that the past and present oppression of blacks is unjust and that God is just, they can only look toward the future for the actualization of black liberation and thereby the manifestation of God's justice and might. But does not black suffering call into question the very presupposition that undergirds the hope for future improvement, namely the justice of God? Consider as well that the suffering of blacks is deserved; where then is the ground and hope for improvement in the black situation?

Let us make the point more explicitly. The employment of eschatological data as a guide to the future condition of blacks requires a specific method if one's position is not to collapse into an improbable and presumptuous hope. The anticipated jubilee cannot be a mere substitute for the absence or paucity of events in the past and present in which the hand of God is at work for black liberation. Otherwise one is endorsing a blatant "pie in the sky" eschatology, and this view is explicitly denounced by each black theologian.

The logical and theological validation of an eschatological approach must proceed as follows: One must move from (a) the actual acts of God in the past or the present or both to (b) conclusions about His character, motives, and mode of activity. Given the principle that God is the sum of His acts, (b) is equivalent to (a), and (a) is thus the primary basis for speaking of (c) God's future activity. In the final analysis, (a) is determinative for (c). What is ruled out is to make (c) determinative for either (a) or (b). This conclusion seems inevitable unless one argues for a radical conversion on the part of God Himself.

I have suggested that the principle that God is the sum of His acts is Sartrean. A strong case, however, can be made for its essential biblical rootage. This is neither the place nor the time to give a lengthy defense of this claim, and the argument does not require it. The reader can confirm it for himself. What I have in mind is suggested by Bernhard Anderson, who concludes, ". . . for Israel to write history was to narrate the mighty acts of the Lord. . . . The Old Testament is the narration of God's action: what He has done, is doing and will do."[13] I contend that the biblical writers establish Who God is by reference to what He has done or is now doing. Their conviction about the nature of God's future acts is grounded in the character of His past and present acts.

It is also important to note that the African concepts of time and history deny normative status to the future. Indeed, when one reflects upon the following passage, one wonders if the eschatological emphasis of much of black religion is one of those areas in which the religion of the slave master has unfortunately usurped the more realistic world view of our African ancestors:

> For the Akamba, Time is . . . simply a composition of events that have occurred, those which are taking place now and those which will *immediately* occur. What has not taken place, or what is unlikely to occur in the immediate future, has no temporal meaning—it belongs to the reality of "no-Time. . . ." From this basic attitude to Time, other important points emerge. The most significant factor is that Time is considered as a two-dimensional phenomenon; with a long "past," and a dynamic "present." The "future" as we know it in the linear conception of Time is virtually non-existent. . . . The future is virtually absent because events which lie in the future have not been realized and cannot, therefore, constitute time which otherwise must be experienced. . . . It is, therefore, what has taken place or will occur shortly that matters much more than what is yet to be.[14]

It is easy now to see how the principle of man as the sum of his acts enlarges the contours of the concept of divine racism. When one makes conclusions about *Who God is* on the basis of *what He has done* for black people, when one accents what is central to the black past—oppression and slavery—as the primary materials for reaching conclusions about the divine attributes, if we do not come to our analysis of the divine nature with the presupposition of His intrinsic goodness for all of mankind but let this conclusion emerge, if at all, on the basis of His actual benevolent acts in behalf of all, it is not difficult to see the category of divine racism surfacing. And when we are forced to make conclusions about God's nature and motives in the light of our subsequent discussion of black suffering as a variety of ethnic suffering, the question Is God a white racist? becomes an even more promising point of departure for black theology.

Toward a Biblical View of Suffering

An examination of the biblical treatment of suffering is necessary at this juncture for several reasons. An understanding of the biblical perspective helps to clarify the relation between suffering and divine racism, particularly the multievidential quality of suffering. It also prepares part of the necessary background for the next section: an analysis of ethnic suffering.

An examination of the biblical understanding of suffering confirms the crucial premise of the multievidentiality of suffering. One can find biblical statements to support each of the logical possibilities—suffering as an expression of (a) divine disfavor or deserved punishment, (b) divine favor, and (c) neither favor nor disfavor. Accordingly, suffering in the biblical view is inherently ambiguous.

No doubt the earliest theory advanced to explain human suffering was that it was invariably punishment for man's sin. Adam and Eve's banishment from Eden, the flood that destroyed all but the house of Noah, the razing of Sodom, etc. illustrate the familiar sequence: human sin, divine punishment, human suffering. Suffering, in this context, is evidence that corrective measures are necessary; suffering demands repentance.

One could easily cite a multitude of other biblical references that express this common response to suffering, but such is not my concern. My purpose is simply to call attention to the variety of interpretations, not to demonstrate that any single explanation is the biblical position. In this way, additional support is marshaled for the theory of the multievidential quality of suffering.

The opposite interpretation, human suffering as evidence of God's favor, also finds expression in the biblical record. ". . . the Lord reproves him whom He loves."[15] One finds similar claims as well in the extracanonical literature, that those who are most pleasing to God have to be tried through suffering. Perhaps the suffering-servant theme, however, is the best and most familiar example of the relation of divine favor and suffering. In contrast to the Deuteronomic theory, in which suffering automatically convicts the sufferer of rebellion and disobedience, the suffering of the servant symbolizes perfect conformity to God's will. Accordingly, corrective measures are not necessary; suffering does not demand repentance. The future holds not judgment but reward and exaltation. In sum, suffering is evidence of more than simply divine favor; it manifests God's highest favor.

Numerous New Testament passages could be cited granting that suffering is not only positive, but a glorious and essential aspect of man's salvation. Peter's first letter is a case in point:

> Beloved, think it not strange concerning the fiery trial which is to try you, as though some strange thing happened unto you: But rejoice, inasmuch as ye are partakers of Christ's sufferings; that, when his glory shall be revealed, ye may be glad also with exceeding joy.[16]

Peter affirms here that suffering is inherent in the life of the Christian, just as it was central to Jesus' own life. Further, that to endure suffering will lead to glory and reward, as it did for Jesus. Elsewhere in the same letter, Peter reminds his readers again: "Forasmuch then as Christ hath suffered for us in the flesh, arm yourselves likewise with the same mind."[17]

Surely it is redundant to labor over those familiar parts of the New Testament record which affirm, at least implicitly, the value of Jesus' suffering and death for man's salvation, or those references to His death and suffering as the highest expression of self-sacrificing love.

The conclusion to be drawn from the foregoing is this: not every instance of suffering is negative in quality and thereby to be attacked or circumvented. Some are not only valuable but necessary for one's salvation.

Other interpretations of suffering cannot be neatly classified as evidence of God's favor or disfavor. Some explanations appear to have a foothold in both camps. Consider those treatments which define suffering as a form of divine warning. Here suffering has a dual role. To suffer indicates on the one hand that the wrong path has been taken. However, suffering can also be regarded as a guide to the proper path in so far as it illuminates the actions to be avoided if man is to obtain his highest good. Moreover, since it is a spur to repentance, it is essential to one's salvation. Thus, suffering as a form of divine warning is easily interpreted as a revelation of divine favor.

The duality of this example reinforces the fundamental point: suffering, in the biblical picture, is ambiguous, and this ambiguity is not dissolved by examining the conspicuous characteristics of suffering.

Other interpretations of suffering express a relation of neither favor nor disfavor. It is possible to affirm that suffering is simply an inherent feature of the human condition; to be human is to suffer, regardless of one's status relative to the divine.[18] Certain sufferings express the elementary truth that man is a creature and not Creator, that he is not all-powerful, in sum, that he is man and not God.

Suffering as God's special method of testing man would also appear to fall into this class. Whether suffering is weal or woe, here depends ultimately upon whether one passes or fails the test. The suffering itself is transparently neutral.

The foregoing analysis underscores the claim that suffering is multievidential; it can embody God's grace, God's curse, or neither. We are thus forced to consider the crucial and difficult question, How do we determine in which class a given instance of suffering belongs; how do we differentiate between the suffering that evinces God's marvelous grace and that which signifies his terrible judgment; how do we determine if the sufferer is an agent of God's salvation or a sinner receiving his rightful punishment? The answer is inescapable: a standard or criteriology for separating negative from positive suffering must be formulated.

This issue is by no means an academic matter, but a core issue, as we shall see, for every theology of liberation.

To reiterate an earlier conclusion: if we define an instance of suffering as positive or necessary for salvation, we are persuaded to endure it. On the other hand, to define suffering as negative is to prepare the ground for its annihilation. It is on the basis of this observation that we affirm the crucial conclusion: a theology of liberation must provide a basis for defining as negative the suffering that is implicit in oppression.

What do the biblical writers propose as the formula for distinguishing between positive and negative suffering? The criterion, I must confess, is not clear-cut. It is easy, for instance, to detect a developing consensus that not all suffering is divine punishment. The consequence of this development, however, is to increase, not reduce, the ambiguity of suffering.

Nonetheless, there is one clear line of thought that enables us to say at least that a given case of suffering is not divine punishment. Obviously, the fact of suffering itself is not sufficient to decide the case. Suffering is present when the sufferer is the recipient of merited punishment, but suffering can also be present when the sufferer is the object of God's favor. Nor does it appear that the special character of suffering, e.g. its severity, requires or permits the removal of one alternative in favor of the other. The differentiating factor must be something other than the suffering itself, even its peculiar characteristics. An analysis of the suffering-servant theme, in my view, supplies the differentiating factor.

The distinguishing element to be noted is a radical shift in the status of the sufferer. This shift, which I will designate as the *exaltation event,* comprises something akin to the principle "from last to first." In the context of oppression, the exaltation event would be labeled the *liberation* event, e.g. the Exodus. An analysis of the servant passages in Isaiah forces the conclusion that two conditions are required to index an individual or group in the class of suffering servant, which is to say, the object of God's favor. There is (1) the fact of suffering and (2) the exaltation-liberation event. If we call (1) the situation of humiliation, then (2) would designate the exaltation or reward. The two events are antithetical. The exaltation event constitutes the elimination of the suffering and its replacement by the opposite state of affairs.

The references "I will divide his portion with the great" and "he shall divide the spoils with the strong"[19] supply the general sense of what is intended in the exaltation event. Even if the exaltation event is postponed to some future time, that is, interpreted eschatologically, it is on the basis of the anticipated event that the present suffering is claimed to be vindicated. Two rhetorical questions summarize the point: Is it possible to declare that Jesus is Lord if we affirm only the Cross and omit the Resurrection? Can we declare that blacks are the suffering servant if the only evidence is the fact of their suffering?

All has not been said on this point. Consider Jeremiah's plaintive question, "Why is my pain perpetual, and my wound incurable?"[20] That the suffering is not replaced by its opposite, that the suffering is unrelieved, triggers the thought of the loss of God's favor in Jeremiah's mind. The book of Job is also illuminating in this connection. Though the epilogue is often considered an editorial addition, I would argue that it is necessary in order to make the text theologically correct. The suffering of Job demands restitution. Job must be vindicated if the interpretation of the prologue—God is testing Job to see if he is a fair-weather friend—is to be distinguished from deserved punishment. And does not this same view lie behind Jesus' own cry from the cross, "My God, my God, why hast thou forsaken me?"[21]

To return to the suffering-servant theme. Another feature points to the necessity of the exaltation event, and if it is missing, the suffering-servant model cannot be legitimately invoked. The suffering servant is claimed to be innocent; his suffering is not deserved punishment. But is it not the exaltation event which substantiates the sufferer's innocence? Without the exaltation event it is not possible to distinguish between the suffering servant and the rank sinner encountering his deserved punishment.

I would also argue, though I stand to be corrected here, that the designation of an individual or group as suffering servant must be executed retrospectively, that is, after the occurrence of the exaltation event. Prior to this event the designation of suffering servant is both gratuitous and without evidential grounds. The interpretation of deserved punishment is equally, if not more, probable.

The importance of this point for an eschatological theodicy cannot be overlooked. The eschatological option, in my view, is a theological dead end, for it leaves the issue unresolved until the distant future. Prior to the exaltation event and given the multievidentiality of suffering, God's favor and disfavor remain equally probable. Only the exaltation event appears to weight the scale for the interpretation of God's favor. Further, one is inclined toward the explanation of divine disfavor or deserved punishment to the degree that the exaltation event tarries.

If the foregoing analysis is correct, to refute the charge of divine racism, according to the biblical model, requires the occurrence of the exaltation-liberation event. And it should be clear that this event of emancipation terminates the suffering implicit in oppression.[22] It is also clear that the identification of this event for *blacks* is no small theological task, particularly if we adhere strictly to the text of Isaiah. The liberation event, according to Isaiah, is not restricted to the eyes of the faithful alone but is visible and acknowledged by the oppressor as well.[23]

In sum, it must be asked if the black theologian can legitimately adopt the suffering-servant model to explain black suffering if he (a) does not isolate in a concrete way the crucial exaltation-liberation event(s) or (b) regards this occurrence as a future event.

Ethnic Suffering and Divine Racism

I have attempted thus far to show that the multievidentiality of suffering, in part, forces consideration of the question, Is God a white racist? At this juncture it is necessary to enlarge the complex of categories that generates the issue of divine racism. The concept of ethnic suffering, the correlate of divine racism, will be our immediate focus.

Four essential features constitute ethnic suffering: (a) maldistribution, (b) negative quality, (c) enormity, and (d) non-catastrophic character. By accenting the ethnic factor I wish to call attention to that suffering which is maldistributed; it is not spread, as it were, more or less randomly and impartially over the total human race. Rather, it is concentrated in a particular ethnic group. My concern in utilizing the concept of ethnic suffering is to accentuate the fact that black suffering is balanced by white non-suffering instead of white suffering. Consequently, black suffering in particular and ethnic suffering in general raise the issue of the scandal of particularity.

John Bowker makes the cogent observation that the problem of the maldistribution of suffering is central in the Old Testament. "The problem in Scripture," he contends, "is not why suffering exists, but why it afflicts some people and not others. The problem is not the *fact* of suffering, but its *distribution*."[24] Ethnic suffering underlines and gives emphasis to the same notion.

If we differentiate between positive and negative suffering, ethnic suffering in my stipulative definition would be a subclass of negative suffering. It describes a suffering without essential value for man's salvation or well-being. It leads away from, rather than toward, one's highest good. In contrast, certain advocates of types of asceticism, for instance, would regard suffering positively, as something to be actively pursued.

A third feature of ethnic suffering is its enormity, and here the reference is to several things: There is the factor of numbers, but numbers in relation to the total class, i.e., the number of suffering Jews or blacks in comparison with the total number of Jews or blacks. The factor of numbers raises the issue of divine racism at the point where the level of suffering and death makes the interpretation of genocide feasible.

Enormity also designates suffering unto death. Ethnic suffering reduces the life expectancy or anticipates the immediate death of the individual. The importance of this feature is that it nullifies various explanations of suffering and thereby narrows the spectrum of possible theodicies. Suffering unto death, for instance, negates any interpretation of pedagogical suffering; i.e., we learn from a burn to avoid fire. This makes little sense if the learning method destroys the learner. Suffering as a form of testing is also contradicted if the amount and severity of the suffering are incommensurate with the alleged purpose. It is for this reason that Rabbi Richard Rubenstein, for instance, denies that the horror of the suffering of Jews at Auschwitz could ever be likened to the testing of Job.[25]

The final feature to be discussed is the non-catastrophic aspect. Ethnic suffering does not strike quickly and then leave after a short and terrible siege. Instead, it extends over long historical eras. It strikes not only the father but the son, the grandson, and the great-grandson. In short, non-catastrophic suffering is transgenerational.

When these aspects of ethnic suffering are connected, one is not tempted to account for their presence on the grounds of the operation of indifferent and impersonal laws of nature. Rather, one is more inclined to explain its causal nexus in terms of purpose and consequently person. This, too, is but a short step to seeing God as perhaps that person.

It is my contention that the peculiarities of black suffering make the *question* of divine racism imperative; it is not my position that the special character of black suffering *answers* the question. What I do affirm is that black theology, precisely because of the prominence of ethnic suffering in the black experience, cannot operate as if the goodness of God for all mankind were a theological axiom.

With the foregoing analysis of ethnic suffering as a background, it is now possible to restate certain aspects of the biblical understanding of suffering. Of special importance in this respect is the connection between the exaltation-liberation event and the catastrophic feature of ethnic suffering. The suffering-servant model, in my view, demands the category of catastrophic suffering; unrelieved suffering or transgenerational suffering appears to contradict it. The interval between Cross and Resurrection was by no means a millennium. Indeed it would be an interesting and rewarding study to examine the duration of suffering in biblical thought when the suffering is not the result of divine disfavor.

A final observation about the limitations of the category of ethnic suffering: The reader, and surely the critic, may sense that ethnic suffering is a self-negating concept. It is possible to argue that ethnic classification is arbitrary and reflects only the operation of human classification. Accordingly it is possible to divide mankind into a mind-boggling variety of ethnic groups to the point where the particularity presupposed in ethnic suffering becomes meaningless. That is, the framework of ethnic suffering permits one to raise the question, Is God a sexist, anti-Semite, anti-Indian, anti-German, anti-Watusi? This is a just criticism and one that should be advanced if the critic thinks it has merit.

Allowing for this problem, the concept, I feel, still warrants consideration. Where one makes the class division is unimportant; nor is it crucial how often the division is made. As long as one is willing to isolate and identify a specific group and demonstrate that it receives a preponderance of suffering in comparison with members outside the class, the issue of the partiality of ultimate reality can be raised. If this is allowed, certain groupings would not meaningfully fall into the camp of ethnic suffering. Given the actual situation of blacks relative to whites in the U.S.A., does it make sense to ask, "Is God a black racist?" on the grounds that whites fit the category of ethnic suffering?

More important from my perspective, however, is the fact that a challenge to the concept of ethnic suffering is actually support for my over-all purpose and argument. It should be recalled that my object is not to demonstrate that God is a white racist or an anti-Semite. Rather, it is to question the theological frameworks within which these charges legitimately surface. Accordingly, to emphasize the self-negating aspect of ethnic suffering is, again, to show the vulnerability of the theological frameworks that are the object of my criticism.

II

WHITE GOD—BLACK PROTEST

A Radical Interpretation of Black Suffering

Despite the prevailing view to the contrary, not all blacks during slavery and reconstruction were convinced that God is righteous, just, and loving. Nor were they persuaded that He would liberate the poor and the weak—especially if they happened to be black. Not all were assured that slavery contradicted God's will and that His plan was ultimately to vindicate black people. Indeed it would be strange if divine racism or its near kin had not suggested itself to our black forebears as the cause of their inhuman plight. Too little attention has been afforded this black protest against God Himself, no doubt because many blacks have found it more comforting, theologically and psychologically, to see themselves as the object of God's boundless love.

We have protested mightily the manner in which whites have glorified Booker T. Washington to the exclusion of more radical black heroes. We have understood the reason for this unpardonable omission: to serve the needs of the white power structure. But we must lodge a similar protest against the failure of blacks themselves to let the impassioned and embittered voices of black protest ring forth with full clarity and strength —even to question God's own honor. This strand of the black religious tradition should no longer be treated like the skeleton in the closet. It must be rescued from the oblivion of a last-chapter status and protected from question-begging attacks that label such indictments against God as anti-religious. This chapter will have served its purpose well if it provides a fresh hearing for this group of black religious protesters.

It would be a mistake to think that this scathing judgment of God's actions and purpose expresses the majority theological opinion of our black ancestors; I acknowledge it does not. But it would also be a capital mistake to conclude that the germ of the charge of divine racism is present only when it is explicitly asserted. I will argue that the same impulse that leads to the affirmation of God's non-existence, to atheism, can also issue in the charge of divine racism.

The primary materials for the discussion are the documents cited by Benjamin Mays in his noted book *The Negro's God as Reflected in His Literature,* but the fact that Mays's work is the most extensive text to examine and collate black thought about God is not the central reason for focusing upon the materials in his work. Rather, the reason is explained by Vincent Harding's Preface to Mays's text:

> It must be said that Mays' documents were often much stronger than his own commentary on them. . . . Next to these works Mays' commentary too often appeared strained and almost inconsequential. This was partly because he sometimes held too rigidly to a mechanistic, socio-psychological mode of analysis which rarely fits well with the understanding of religion. So terms like "compensatory," "security," and "social reconstruction" were repeated constantly without moving a reader to the depths and ambiguities of the religious experience being examined.[1]

Harding's point is that the documents could appropriately

yield a different—and more significantly, a more radical—interpretation. My purpose here is to supply that interpretation. I seek to demonstrate that the documents in fact raise the question, Is God a white racist?—a question that does not appear on the pages of Mays's book. In this way, a purpose already initiated is advanced: to show that though the term divine racism is perhaps novel, the ideas and arguments that underlie it are not.

Countee Cullen

Our discussion focuses upon the materials Mays utilizes to illustrate "ideas of God involving frustration, doubt, God's impotence and His non-existence."[2] It is not difficult to show that the themes of frustration, doubt, etc. are also the roots of the charge of divine racism. Consider, for example, the following lines from Countee Cullen's *Color.*

> Wishing He I served were black,
> Thinking then it would not lack
> Precedent of pain to guide it,
> Let who would or might deride it,
> Surely then this flesh would know
> Yours had borne a kindred woe.
> Lord I fashion dark gods, too,
> Daring even to give you
> Dark despairing features where,
> Crowned with dark rebellious hair,
> Patience wavers just so much as
> Mortal grief compels, while touches
> Quick and hot, of anger, rise
> To smitten cheek and weary eyes.
> Lord, forgive me if my need
> Sometimes shapes a human creed.[3]

The suggestion here is that God is not black, but white; and because He is not black, He is either indifferent or less sympathetic to black needs than He would be if His color were a darker hue. There is, then, an obvious connection between God's color and the character of His actions and attitudes relative to blacks.

But the center of Cullen's argument connects blackness and suffering. God does not treat blacks as He should, because He Himself is not black. If God were black, Cullen contends, He, too, like black humanity, would be a sufferer. And this would make Him more empathic to suffering blacks. Blacks and God would be true soul brothers, because their conditions would be identical, i.e. overwhelming misery. The implicit premise here is that if God were black, then black suffering would cease. Hence, the continued misery of blacks is indisputable evidence that God is not black. Hence also, the necessity of making God in the image of the black worshiper—color Him black.

The same theme of blackness and suffering informs other works of Cullen. I would conclude that the initial lines of the following poem are ironic and thus must be interpreted as contrary to the final line.

> I doubt not God is good, well-meaning, kind,
> And did He stoop to quibble could tell why
> The little buried mole continues blind,
> Why flesh that mirrors Him must some day die,
> . . . Inscrutable His ways are, and immune
> To catechism by a mind too strewn
> With petty cares to slightly understand
> What awful brain compels His awful hand.
> Yet do I marvel at this curious thing:
> To make a poet black, and bid him sing.[4]

A single argument shines through these lines clearly: to be black is to be a sufferer, and thus the incongruity, yea, the self-contradiction of a black muse. A sufferer should mourn, wail, and cry, but not sing and rejoice. And though he surmises that the mortality of man and the inexplicable cruelties and inequities in nature are somehow compatible with the goodness of God's inscrutable will, the black poet stands out as the ultimate theological scandal and obscenity.

The same ironic note is present in "Pagan Prayer." Here Cullen argues that blacks should accept the traditional concept of God only when black suffering is terminated. That is to say, after the liberation-exaltation event. He says in effect that he will not believe until the suffering of blacks is no more. I do not understand him to mean all suffering but only that suffering which lies at the core of oppression. And in the light of other works, e.g. *The Black Christ,* I receive the impression that he doubts that liberation will in fact occur. And is this not a tacit admission that God is not for black people?

> Not for myself I make this prayer,
> But for this race of mine
> That stretches forth from shadowed places
> Dark hands for bread and wine.
>
> For me, my heart is pagan mad,
> My feet are never still,
> But give them hearths to keep them warm
> In homes high on a hill.
>
> For me, I pay my debts in kind,
> And see no better way.
> Bless those who turn the other cheek
> For love of you and pray.
>
> Our Father, God; our Brother, Christ,
> Or are we bastard kin,
> That to our plaints your ears are closed,
> Your doors barred from within?
>
> Our Father, God; our Brother, Christ,
> Retrieve my race again;
> So shall you compass this black sheep,
> This pagan heart. Amen.[5]

Cullen's *The Black Christ* is the most helpful segment of

his thought for the particular focus of this investigation. This poem vividly illustrates that the dehumanizing situation of blacks that invites the charge of divine racism can also lead to the acceptance of atheism, agnosticism, or humanism as appropriate religious options. In addition, *The Black Christ* throws light upon the logical affinity of black atheism and black humanism, and these, in turn, with the affirmation of divine racism.

Certain prefatory remarks are necessary to provide an appropriate framework for interpreting this work as well as identifying my approach to it. The prologue to this extended poem identifies its character. It is the account of a radical conversion, of "how one man who cursed Christ's name"[6] finally acknowledges that it is the same Christ who has redeemed him. I will identify this figure in the analysis as "the blasphemer." Interspersed throughout the poem are significant remarks by the blasphemer that reflect his thought prior to his conversion. Accordingly, these remarks, which are the focus of my analysis, should not be regarded as Cullen's definitive position.

It must also be noted that Cullen's agenda, as in the other poems cited, is to account for the persistence and ruthlessness of black suffering. In the language of the concept of ethnic suffering, his matter of interest is the non-catastrophic character of black suffering. Three explanations are advanced in the poem. On the one hand, unrelieved black suffering is explicable if there is no God, i.e. atheism. As the figure Jim affirms, "Likely there ain't no God at all."[7]

The two remaining solutions to the enigma of black suffering presuppose the opposite conclusion: God exists. Black suffering can be made intelligible if God exists but is not active in human affairs. "Your God is somewhere worlds away. . . . O He has weightier things to do than lavish time on me and you."[8] Finally, one can resolve the riddle of black suffering if God exists and is active in certain sectors of human history but absents Himself from the struggle for black liberation. The elimination of black oppression is not a priority item on God's agenda—

if it is found there at all. This alternative clearly suggests that
God is a white racist:

> God, if He was, kept to His skies,
> And left us to our enemies.
>
> . . . .
>
> A man was lynched last night.
> "Why?" Jim would ask, his eyes star-bright.
> "A white man struck him; he showed fight.
> Maybe God thinks such things are right."[9]

And God apparently thinks such things are right, because they
occur repeatedly, and He does nothing to prevent them or
avenge them.

Nor does Jesus, regarded here as "the white Christ," escape
the scorn of the blasphemer:

> But Christ who conquered Death and Hell,
> What has He done for you who spent
> A bleeding life for His content?
> Or is the white Christ, too, distraught
> By these dark sins His Father wrought?[10]

One should note here Cullen's stubborn emphasis that only
the occurrence of the liberation-exaltation event is sufficient
evidence for affirming God's favorable disposition toward
blacks. In fact he appears to suggest that the absence of this
event substantiates that God is against blacks. Jesus' power is
unmistakable, according to Cullen, in His victory over death.
Thus His failure to exert the same power in behalf of blacks
must be regarded not as an indication of His impotence but
an admission that He does not want to. Indeed the final line
intimates that Christ regrets God's creation of blacks; better
that blacks had never been born is Christ's spirit.

When we consider Cullen's contrast between ancient and
contemporary Gods, we encounter another implicit charge of
divine racism. The Gods of old requested worship and praise
only because They had successfully satisfied the essential needs
of Their worshipers and corrected the miserable conditions of

Their followers. And again the accent is upon the satisfaction of needs here and now, not in the future:

> When Rome was a suckling, when Greece was young,
> Then there were Gods fit to be sung,
> Who paid the loyal devotee
> For service rendered zealously,
> In coin a man might feel and spend,
> Not marked "Deferred to Journey's End."
> The servant then was worth his hire;
> He went unscathed through flood and fire;
> Gods were a thing then to admire.
> "Bow down and worship us," they said.
> "You shall be clothed, be housed and fed,
> While yet you live, not when you're dead.
> Strong are our arms where yours are weak.
> On them that harm you will we wreak
> The vengeance of a God though they
> Were Gods like us in every way.
> Not merely is an honor laid
> On those we touch with our accolade;
> We strike for you with that same blade!"[11]

Several points are worth noting in the foregoing description. The ancient Gods, Cullen argues, make plain how God would act if He were, in fact, favorably disposed toward blacks. The condition of blacks would be turned right side up, and thus humanized. Nor should the avenging might of God be over-looked. This, according to Cullen, is the only appropriate relation between God and man. Anything less is unworthy of the label "religion." In advancing this viewpoint Cullen is actually making the liberation-exaltation event the core of religious faith.

It is helpful to view the latter conclusion in light of another declaration of Cullen's: a God who does not usher in the liberation event is tantamount to no God at all. And here we see close up the logical connection between the charge of divine racism and the affirmation of atheism:

Rebellion barked now like a gun;
Like a split dam, this faith in one
Who in my sight had never done
One extraordinary thing
That I should praise his name, or sing
His bounty and his grace, let loose
The pent-up torrent of abuse
That clamored in me for release:
"Nay I have done with deities
Who keep me ever on my knees,
My mouth forever in a tune
Of praise, yet never grant the boon
Of what I pray for night and day.
God is a toy; put Him away."[12]

Better, then, to create your own God; what have you lost?

"Or make you one of wood or stone
That you can call your very own,
A thing to feel and touch and stroke,
Who does not break you with a yoke
Of iron that he whispers soft;
Nor promise you fine things aloft
While back and belly here go bare,
While His own image walks so spare
And finds this life so hard to live
You doubt that He has aught to give.
Better an idol shaped of clay
Near you, than one so far away.
Although it may not heed your labors
At least it will not mind your neighbors".
"In His own time, He will unfold
You milk and honey, streets of gold,
High walls of jasper . . ." phrases rolled
Upon the tongues of idiots.
What profit *then*, if hunger gluts us *now?*[13]

A superior way lies beyond the horizon of creating new deities: look upon oneself as God.

> Better my God should be
> This moving, breathing frame of me,
> Strong hands and feet, live heart and eyes;
> And when these close, say then God dies.[14]

Cullen is not arguing here for the deification of man. We must recall the function of God in the previous discussion: to satisfy man's basic needs here and now. Thus his meaning is more this: man in general and black man in particular must look to himself as the only source of salvation. The ultimate agent of human salvation is man himself.

We have noted how the blasphemer intertwines the charge of divine racism and God's non-existence. But his preference leans toward atheism. The reason for this choice is worth examining, for it helps to explain a curious phenomenon. Black voices of protest—others will be considered in the next section—are more than willing to endorse atheism, but divine racism is not mentioned nearly as often. The materials, however, logically support both viewpoints. The difference between an interpretation of atheism and divine racism is not a difference in the evidence; the point of departure for both is the scandal of ethnic suffering. What occurs is that the premise of divine racism is smothered by a crucial and question-begging presupposition: benevolence is intrinsic to the concept of God.

As Jim acknowledges, "God could not be, if He deemed right the grief that ever met our sight."[15] Clearly a racist God is theologically impossible where God's universal benevolence is presupposed. Having assumed God's intrinsic goodness and justice, only two alternatives remain: adopt a theodicy based on God's benevolence, or opt for atheism.

But atheism, when it emerges in the context of ethnic suffering, is the twin of divine racism. Between the two there is not only a continuity of purpose, but also a common strategy and similar theological entailments. Each attacks the available theodicies with the view in mind of eliminating them from theological consideration. Each attempts to accomplish this by presenting counterevidence that the extant theodicies cannot assimilate. For both, worship of God is effectively eliminated, and each would conclude that blacks must pursue their liberation without hope of extrahuman or supernatural support. Each, in sum, collapses into some variety of humanism.

Some readers of Cullen will question the accuracy of the foregoing interpretation and point to the fact that the blasphemous one repents and recants. He who chided "the white Christ" now praises Him.

> . . . I who mouthed my blasphemies . . .
> Am found forever on my knees,
> Ever to praise her Christ with her,
> Knowing He can at will confer
> Magic on miracle to prove
> And try me when I doubt His love.[16]

One point, however, must be underscored: the reason for the blasphemer's radical conversion. He believes because the miracle of miracles occurs, a foreshadowing of the liberation event. A black man is saved from the howling lynch mob and returns, as it were, from the dead, resurrected like Christ Himself:

> "No more," I cried, "this is too much
> For one mad brain to stagger through."
> For he stood in utmost view
> Whose death I had been witness to;
> But now he breathed; he lived, he walked;
> His tongue could speak my name; he talked.
> He questioned me to know what art
> Had made his enemies depart.[17]

But is not the cause of this radical conversion the very prerequisites for belief set forth in "Pagan Prayer"? He will believe, once the concrete situation of blacks is improved. Thus, in my view, there is a rigid coherence in the various layers of Cullen's thought. Divine racism and atheism are dispelled only by the occurrence of black liberation. The blasphemer's conversion

is the consequence of a black resurrection; Christ appears, as
it were, in a black form. A concrete instance of black deliverance is manifest. In sum, to refute ethnic suffering, one must
point to concrete events of black liberation.

By way of comparison, it is helpful to survey several black
religionists who retain their belief in the God of the Judaeo-
Christian tradition. In this way, the precise points of difference
between them and Cullen's blasphemer can be identified. The
thought of the Reverend Nathaniel Paul and Bishop Daniel A.
Payne serve this purpose well.

Paul addresses the same tabooed and perplexing question
to God that Du Bois voiced:

> And, oh thou immaculate God, be not angry with us,
> while we come into this thy sanctuary, and make the
> bold inquiry in this thy holy temple, why it was that thou
> didst look on with the calm indifference of an uncon-
> cerned spectator, when thy holy law was violated, thy
> divine authority despised and a portion of thine own
> creatures reduced to a state of mere vassalage and
> misery?[18]

And as with Cullen's blasphemer, the continued oppression
of blacks can only signify the non-existence of God. Here
again we see the prevailing theological inclination of Christian
thought to knit together God's existence and benevolence so
tightly that any attack upon the latter undermines the former
as well:

> Did I believe that [slavery] would always continue, and
> man to the end of time would be permitted with impunity
> to usurp the same undue authority over his fellows . . .
> I would deny the superintending power of divine Provi-
> dence in the affairs of this life; I would ridicule the re-
> ligion of the Saviour of the World, and treat as the worst
> of men the ministers of the everlasting Gospel; I would
> consider my bible as a book of false and delusive fables,
> and commit it to flame; Nay, I would still go further; I

would at once confess myself an atheist, and deny the existence of a holy God.[19]

Wherein lies the difference between Cullen's blasphemer and Paul? For both, the fact of ethnic suffering is a clear contradiction of God's justice and goodness. Both establish the same condition as proof that God is holy and just: the liberation of the black oppressed. On this point Paul is explicit:

The progress of emancipation, though slow, is nevertheless certain: It is certain because that God who has made of one blood all nations of men . . . has so decreed; I therefore have no hesitation in declaring from this sacred place that not only throughout the United States of America but throughout every part of the habitable world where slavery exists, it will be abolished. . . .[20]

The crucial difference appears to be that Paul is more futuristic; he permits an eschatological confirmation of God's goodness to a degree that is not apparent in Cullen's blasphemer.[21] According to the latter, as long as the definitive liberation event is postponed, final judgment regarding God's love and justice must also be postponed.

Bishop Payne's position parallels that of Paul; the oppressive condition, i.e. ethnic suffering, also compels him to question God's existence. Payne avoids the quicksand of atheism because he, like Paul, was convinced that slavery and oppression would be annihilated in the future by God's mighty hand:

. . . I began to question the existence of God, and to say: "If he does exist, is he just? If so, why does he suffer one race to oppress and enslave another, to rob them by unrighteous enactments of rights, which they hold most dear and sacred?" . . . Again said I: "Is there no God?" But then there came into my mind those solemn words: "With God one day is as a thousand years and a thousand years as one day. Trust in him and he will bring slavery and all its outrages to an end.[22]

Miscellaneous Voices of Black Protest

Other black thinkers evidence features of the charge of divine racism. James Baldwin's religious odyssey involved a passage through the conviction that God is white and a racist, and it is his recognition of the centrality of ethnic suffering that impels him to this conclusion. "But God—and I felt this even then, so long ago—is white. . . . If his love was so great, and if he loved all his children, why were we, the blacks, cast down so far? Why?"[23]

Carter G. Woodson introduces yet another nuance to the charge of divine racism, and the methodological implications of his analysis are crucial for black theology. He correctly calls attention to the inclination in Western thought to see benevolence as intrinsic to God. The consequence of this is to see Him as active in human affairs only where good is present. Evil and misery are seldom traced to Him. Woodson, however, wants to assign both good and evil to God. And if evil is related to the black condition, there is the obvious implication of divine racism:

> [Rural Negroes] laugh at those who doubt the existence of an all-seeing Providence. . . . The Lord has delivered these Negroes from too many trials and tribulations for them to doubt His power or His interest in mankind. God is not held responsible for the Negroes being carried away captive to be slaves of white men; God has nothing to do with their long persecution and the intolerable conditions under which they have to live, but great praise should be given Him for permitting them to exist under the circumstances. The evils from which these Negroes suffer, they believe, resulted from the sin of their forefathers and their own shortcomings.[24]

God, in sum, cannot be the cause of black misery, because of the conviction of His inherent benevolence for all mankind. Thus the tendency to assign ultimate responsibility for the crimes of human history to man, even blacks themselves. We note again the presupposition that if God is, He is good.

One final voice must be heard: Nella Larsen's novel *Quicksand*. The reason is both personal and polemical. Some of the passages describe what would have been the content of my own diary of theological development. It also illustrates a different logical progression, which supports the previously discussed point regarding the identity of sources for divine racism and atheism. The sequence in the following passage is from (a) the conviction that black suffering confirms God's nonexistence to (b) black suffering implies that God is a white racist:

> In that period of racking pain and calamitous fright Helga had learned what passion and credulity could do to one. In her was born angry bitterness and an enormous disgust. The cruel, unrelieved suffering had beaten down her protective wall of artificial faith in the infinite wisdom, in the mercy of God. For had she not called in her agony on Him? And He had not heard. Why? Because she knew now, He wasn't there. Didn't exist. Into that yawning gap of unspeakable brutality had gone, too, her belief in the miracle and wonder of life. . . . Life wasn't a miracle, a wonder. It was, for Negroes at least, only a great disappointment. Something to be got through with as best one could. No one was interested in them or helped them. God! Bah! And they were only a nuisance to other people. . . . The white man's God. —And His great love for all people regardless of race! What idiotic nonsense she had allowed herself to believe. How could she, how could anyone, have been so deluded? How could ten million black folk credit it when daily before their eyes was enacted its contradiction?

> . . . And this, Helga decided, was what ailed the whole Negro race in America, this fatuous belief in the white man's God, this childlike trust in full compensation for all woes and privations in "Kingdom Come." Sary Jones'

absolute conviction, "In de nex worl' we's all recompense," came back to her. And ten million souls were as sure of it as was Sary. How the white man's God must laugh at the great joke He had played on them. Bound them to slavery, then to poverty and insult, and made them bear it unresistingly, uncomplainingly almost, by sweet promises of mansions in the sky by and by.[25]

Larsen's description here is reminiscent of Bertrand Russell's portrayal of a demonic God who utilizes religion and human suffering as the basis for a gigantic cosmic joke.[26] In Larsen's account, however, it is only the black man who bears the brunt of God's demonic humor, and this additional factor of particularity suggests white racism rather than God's malice or misanthropy.

We note as well in Larsen's account the same complex of factors that are now familiar to the reader: putting God in the docket because of the continued oppression of blacks, and the ridicule of attempts to legitimate and rationalize present black suffering on the grounds of alleged release from suffering in the future. The concept of God as the sum of His acts is also presupposed here in so far as it is argued that blacks have reached conclusions about God that clearly contradict their own existential situation.

III

SHOULD A PRIEST CALL A DOCTOR?
THEODICY, OPPRESSION, AND QUIETISM

Belief Regulates Action

Long ago Plato declared that we act on the basis of what we believe to be true about the fundamental categories of theology and philosophy: the nature of God or Ultimate Reality, of man, etc. He further stated that if our beliefs are inaccurate or unsound, our actions invariably will be inauthentic.

More recently Benjamin Mays called attention to the same reciprocal dependence between belief and action. The major argument of *The Negro's God* establishes that the characteristic activity of blacks in the social arena—specifically, whether they conform or rebel—is controlled ultimately by the particular concept of God they embrace. As he puts it succinctly, the Negro's "social philosophy and his idea of God go hand in hand."[1] Mays's category of "compensatory beliefs" presupposes the same viewpoint. It seeks to identify those theological beliefs which "enable Negroes to endure hardship, suffer pain and withstand maladjustment, but . . . do not necessarily motivate them to strive to eliminate the source of the ills they suffer."[2] Thus his purpose reduces to the isolation and then the elimination of the theological concepts that, if accepted, reconcile the believer to his oppression.

In this connection it is instructive to cite a particular example of a compensatory belief from Mays's text. The example that bears repeating is the "harder the Cross, [the] brighter the crown" theodicy. Central to this belief is the conviction that the Negro is God's chosen vessel and that his suffering is God's means of disciplining him for his divine task. His suffering, then, is the sign that God is "bringing him out victoriously and triumphantly in the end. . . . Believing this about God, the Negro . . . has stood back and suffered much without bitterness, without striking back and without trying aggressively to realize to the full his needs in this world."[3]

Recent theologians and philosophers of liberation endorse the same viewpoint.[4] Oppression, they contend, is maintained and vitalized by a specific set of beliefs about man and the larger reality in which he lives. At the base of oppression lies a complex of beliefs that define the role and status of the oppressor and the oppressed, and this same complex of beliefs legitimates both. The oppressed, in part, are oppressed precisely because they buy, or are indoctrinated to accept, a set of beliefs that negate those attitudes and actions necessary for liberation. Accordingly, the purpose and first step of a theology of liberation is to effect a radical conversion of the mind of the oppressed, to free his mind from those destructive and enslaving beliefs that stifle the movement toward liberation.[5]

The specific purpose of this chapter, to use Mays's terminology, is to analyze the compensatory aspects of various theodicies. The reader should understand that I am not arguing that every theodicy is compensatory and counterrevolutionary. In fact, I will identify in due course the outline of a theodicy that leads away from quietism and oppression. My concern at this juncture is to isolate those treatments of

black suffering which the black theologian must avoid—if his
system is to serve as a viable theology of liberation.

Theodicy: Prop for Oppression

The reader will quickly note that the discussion draws
upon the thought of Albert Camus, and certain explanatory
comments are necessary regarding the utilization of his works.
Let me say in advance that the argument attributed to Camus
here is not explicitly set forth in any of his writings. I have
reconstructed an argument based on some intriguing leads
and insights from *The Plague* primarily and, to a lesser degree, *The Rebel*. I am confident, however, that nothing affirmed here is contrary to Camus's thought. It must also be
asserted that the basic conclusion I wish to extract from
Camus—that at the heart of oppression is a statement of
theodicy, usually one that entails quietism—can also be dis-
tilled from the theologians and philosophers of liberation
already cited. I have concentrated on Camus simply because
his argument is the more detailed, cogent, interesting, and
easily accessible to the general reader.

By way of introduction to Camus's argument, it is necessary to make some general observations about his over-all
purpose and method. This will involve some generalizations
about oppression, quietism, and their interrelation.

The Plague is a literary portrayal of authentic and inauthentic responses to human suffering in particular and the
human situation in general. The inauthentic responses, on
the whole, are accounts of theodicies with a long history in
the Judaeo-Christian tradition. This tradition, Camus concludes, has unfortunately adopted an understanding of human
suffering that supports oppression. It fosters a spirit of conformity to human sufferings that ought to be obliterated; it
ultimately leads to quietism—if it is consistent. Thus Camus's
real purpose is to destroy the force of those theodicies which
breed quietism and thereby sustain oppression. His purpose

becomes clearer when we see it in the light of some general observations about oppression and quietism.

An earlier argument concluded that oppression is reducible to a form of negative suffering. This is to say that to assign a positive character to suffering dictates that we embrace and endure it; to regard it as negative motivates us to crush it. Accordingly, to define a situation as oppressive demands that we first label the suffering implicit in that situation as negative.

To move the argument one step further: whatever impedes the characterization of that suffering as negative, constitutes an essential prop for oppression. If a theological or philosophical concept serves to make suffering neutral or, even worse, an essential ingredient of one's salvation, it provides, at the same time, substantial support for the world view of oppression.

From this vantage point the strategy of a theology of liberation is clearly focused. The oppressed must withhold their allegiance and conformity to the existing institutions and structures of oppression; they must jettison the beliefs and concepts that give oppression its moral and conceptual justification; ultimately they must seek a realignment of power. They must, in short, rebel. But if the elimination of oppression requires rebellion, the stimulation of rebellion demands an interpretation that classifies the suffering involved in oppression as dehumanizing.

Once the purpose of theodicy is recognized, its alliance with oppression is further exposed. The aim of theodicy in Christian thought has been to exonerate God's purpose and governance in the face of some questionable and embarrassing features of the human condition. Its goal, in other terms, has been to rob suffering of its pernicious flavor. This is the import of Camus's charge that the Gospels vindicate in advance human suffering and death. This is also what Marx, before him, meant in speaking of religion as an "opiate." Marx, no doubt, would have been on safer grounds had he defined theodicy, rather than religion per se, as an opiate.

To make the same point from another perspective: theodicy leads ultimately to quietism, to the acceptance of one's own suffering and that of others. To explain this point necessitates that we discuss the meaning of quietism. I find the usual equation of quietism and "doing nothing" totally unacceptable. Is it not the case that "doing nothing" is always reducible to "doing something," a concrete activity? We come closer to the heart of quietism if we interpret it as a choice to *act* in a certain way. Namely, it is to choose to act in a way that preserves and conserves what is already present; quietism, in the final analysis, collapses into a posture of conformity. From another side, quietism is the refusal to undertake corrective action, especially where basic cultural practices and institutional structures are at issue. "Thus the fundamental distinction between quietism and its opposite is not that between activity and doing nothing, but rather conformity as opposed to rebellion relative to the status quo."[6]

I would advance another observation about quietism: it is the consequence of a particular set of beliefs about the nature of man, ultimate reality, and man's salvation. For instance, if one concludes that corrective activity is *unnecessary*, quietism is the result. We reach this conclusion whenever we are convinced that the ideal is already present or in the process of being realized. Corrective action is also deemed unnecessary if we believe that the actions necessary to produce the ideal have already been initiated or will be completed by some other agent, e.g. God.

I would also argue that one is pushed toward quietism if he is persuaded that remedial action is *impossible;* that is to say, it will not be successful. Only if suicide is my purpose, will I knowingly defy the law of gravity. An act is labeled impossible when man encounters an apparently invincible force or when rectification necessitates the modification of some ultimate structure of reality or human nature. Note, for instance, the quietist implications of the maxim "You can't change human nature."

Finally, quietism is the normal response to the conviction

that corrective action is *inappropriate*. If I believe that the proposed remedy will cause more harm than the disease, I am obviously not inclined to utilize it.

A Summary of Camus's Critique of Christian Theodicy

Having described the connection between oppression and quietism, it is now possible to outline the structure of Camus's argument. We must keep in mind that his examination of suffering actually constitutes a frontal attack on Christian theodicies, with the view in mind of establishing their invalidity. To eliminate oppression, he concludes, the theodicies that are its foundation must first be rooted out. And he seeks to destroy their force by demonstrating that Christian theodicy ultimately collapses into quietism, which most Christians would regard as theologically and morally reprehensible. Consequently, to avoid the strait jacket of quietism, the extant Christian theodicies must be scrapped.

Camus's critique is accomplished fictionally through the actions and thoughts of Father Panaloux, a Jesuit priest, and we become aware of his theological position through two sermons. The first is preached at the onset of the plague, the second during its climax. The two sermons, for Camus, appear to comprise the end points of the spectrum of theodicies formulated in the Judaeo-Christian tradition. It must be emphasized, however, that the two sermons are the necessary background and introduction for Camus's main argument, namely the alleged connection between Christian theodicy and quietism. The latter discussion is concentrated in the period after the second sermon, and this particular arrangement of the materials leads one to conclude that Camus is addressing a pointed challenge to the Christian theologian. The two sermons, he seems to say, comprise the spectrum of possible resolutions of human suffering acceptable to the Christian in the past, but both points of the spectrum lead to the same position: quietism. Camus also appears to say that the Christian community has not recognized the quietist implications of its understanding of human suffering, and consequently an adequate response has not yet emerged. I also hear Camus announcing between the lines that the attempt to accommodate the challenge of quietism will push Christian theology perilously close to the position of humanism, which he endorses.[7]

It must also be indicated that though the sermons are inherently different in various respects, they agree totally on this basic point: suffering, whatever its character, cannot count decisively against the benevolence of God. Both, in short, presuppose God's intrinsic and ultimate goodness. It is this presupposition that Camus attacks most forcibly, and it, accordingly, will be the primary focus of the subsequent investigation.

The logical character of the two sermons is different, and this must be noted. The first sermon adopts a *demonstrative* approach to theodicy. Panaloux affirms that the resolution of human suffering is capable of deductive certainty and empirical validation. He allows further that a theodicy can be substantiated by reference to *objective* certainties; the principle that truth is subjectivity does not regulate the discipline of theodicy.

Having described the essentials of demonstrative theodicies, Camus then proceeds to invalidate them. Once this is accomplished, Camus moves to consider and invalidate the opposite approach, theodicies of *last resort*. This variety is similar to the Kierkegaardian category of "the leap of faith." Theodicies of last resort, he argues next, collapse either into the "beyond human comprehension" theodicy or its near kin, the "beyond human history," or eschatological, theodicy. The final plank of Camus's argument is to demonstrate that both the theodicy of last resort and the demonstrative theodicy open the door to quietism.

Camus appears to follow Kierkegaard's logical strategy here. He first demolishes those positions which incorporate the norm "truth is objectivity" in religion and Christian faith. By this procedure he successfully clears the field for those positions which consciously adopt the opposite principle, "truth is subjectivity." Indeed, one can correctly view the progression from the first to the second sermon as an effort to establish the subjectivity of truth as normative for theodicy in particular and theology in general.

A Demonstrative Theodicy

With the foregoing as background, the content of the first sermon may now claim our attention. Panaloux's opening remarks affirm that the plague, i.e. human suffering, introduces the theodicy question for the Christian. Human misery clamors for a theological account that justifies the afflictions men encounter. To this end the first sermon is directed. Panaloux's essential apologia is that human suffering is totally consistent with God's love and righteousness, His judgment and salvation. Man, moreover, can substantiate this logical harmony; no appeal to a faith principle is necessary. Human suffering can be explained in accord with the common human categories of morality and rationality. Human suffering does not constitute a theological scandal; there is no *problem* of evil per se.

Panaloux makes this clear by advancing several theological explanations of human suffering. The primary account sees suffering on the one hand as divine punishment and judgment, on the other as an aspect of God's saving work. The two are related like two sides of the same coin. There can be no doubt, according to Panaloux, that the plague is merited punishment for prior sins. Tracing the history of the plague in the Bible, he observes that the plague first appears as an instrument used by God to strike down His enemies. Yet, at the same time, it winnows out His chosen. The plague is "the flail of God, and the world His threshing floor, and implacably He will thresh out His harvest until the wheat is separated from the chaff."[8]

Panaloux concedes that to verify that deserved punishment is the cause of the plague demands that only the wicked can be afflicted. This is to affirm, as Job's friends did, that the fact of suffering is *prima facie* evidence of the sufferer's prior sin. But Panaloux also wants to affirm that the judgment and punishment of the sufferer aids the salvation of those unaffected by the plague. The plague warns us that God does not apathetically overlook our iniquities. The horror of the plague in our midst, thus, motivates us to repent and conform to His will. We are given, as it were, a second chance for salvation. Finally, the plague illuminates and underscores man's impotence and crucifies his arrogance and specious self-sufficiency. In this way, man is humbly prepared for the necessity and acceptance of God's saving grace.

A Theodicy of Last Resort

The second sermon stands in stark contrast to the first, though both insist that suffering, regardless of its quality, is consistent with God's boundless love. But here the similarity ends. The first sermon demonstrated this conclusion by means of objective certainties. Panaloux's opening theodicy repels neither man's reason nor his conscience.

By contrast, the second sermon is a theodicy of last resort. We should not conclude, however, that it is superior to its rival, as if it were the final victor in a gladiatorial contest of theological alternatives. The more appropriate metaphor is that of "a drowning man in a stormy sea who seizes the nearest plank, knowing that whether he sinks or swims with it, it is the best that he has."[9] Or that of a spinster who settles for an unattractive suitor because to decline his offer is to be condemned to spinsterhood. The theodicy of the second sermon rests not on a foundation of objective certainties, but subjective uncertainties; it is a leap of faith into the unknown.

The reason for this radical shift in approach is a crucial event that stands between the two sermons. A small child, whom Panaloux describes as "innocent," dies a horrible death in spite of Panaloux's own prayers and the valiant medical efforts of Dr. Rieux. The death of the innocent child flagrantly contradicts the demonstration of the first sermon. That suffering is deserved punishment can no longer be maintained in the face of the innocent's death. The plague has struck down the guiltless, and any error in the plague's ability to discriminate between the wheat and the chaff calls into question the theodicy of deserved punishment. The death of the innocent comprises a theological scandal, for it appears to be unassimilable in the demonstrative theodicies. Panaloux is unequivocal on this point: "In other manifestations of life God has made things easy for us, . . . but relative to the plague he puts us, so to speak, with our backs to the wall."[10]

Camus expresses the point in another way; he calls attention to a shift in Panaloux's preaching style. The pronoun "you" dominates the first sermon, because Panaloux regards himself as "wheat" and his audience as "chaff." After the scandal event, the death of the young child, Panaloux now speaks of "we," for the neat distinction between "wheat" and "chaff" has collapsed; he can no longer be certain in which group he belongs.

In this connection it is instructive to examine the explanations of suffering Panaloux dismisses as inadequate and inappropriate. First, the eschatological theodicy is not acceptable, for it balances a known suffering, an actual event, with an anticipated event whose actuality and commensurate quality are both problematical:

> Father Panaloux refused to have recourse to simple devices. . . . He might easily have assured them that the child's sufferings would be compensated for by an eternity of bliss awaiting him. But how could he give that assurance when, to tell the truth, he knew nothing about it? But who would dare to assert that eternal happiness can compensate for a single moment of human suffering?[11]

A related argument from *The Rebel* is pertinent here. Camus questions the "beyond human history" account of suffering on the grounds that it is not in fact a justification, for it does

not actually indicate how the suffering fits into God's ultimate
plan. The eschatological resolution merely postpones the alleged justification to a future date. This approach assumes
that the end, God's plan for mankind, justifies the suffering
experienced in the present. But the good or evil quality of
God's blueprint remains uncertain and unclear until the use
of that suffering is substantiated. What the eschatological
approach provides, according to Camus, is not a justification
but a "tragic hope."

Another observation on this issue merits mention: The
eschatological resolution has value for theodicy only because
it presupposes God's intrinsic benevolence, thus concluding
that the present, which is bad, will be replaced by a future
bliss. But is not this presupposition question-begging and
gratuitous in the light of the multievidential character of
suffering and the charge of divine racism?

It is also illuminating that John Hick, the most recent
advocate of an eschatological theodicy, acknowledges that it
involves an unresolved mystery:

> Our "solution" then to this baffling problem of excessive
> and undeserved suffering is a frank appeal to the posi-
> tive value of mystery. Such suffering remains unjust and
> inexplicable, haphazard and cruelly excessive. The mys-
> tery . . . is a real mystery, impenetrable to the ration-
> alizing human mind. It challenges Christian faith with
> its utterly baffling, alien, destructive meaninglessness.[12]

Make no mistake, Camus wishes to force this conclusion
upon the Christian. When confronted with the scandal of
human or ethnic suffering, he must recognize and acknowledge that the route of logical demonstration and empirical
verification is closed—particularly if he covets an eschatological theodicy. Citing the Resurrection, Jesus' identification
with the poor, etc. do not provide a theological detour around
this road block, for as Camus's inverted analysis of Golgotha
certified, these events are also multievidential.

Confronted with the scandal event, the Christian, Panaloux

concludes, has the choice either "to love God or to hate God." What these inescapable alternatives entail is unmasked when we consider Panaloux's description of what it means to love God:

> The love of God is a hard love. It demands total self-surrender . . . and yet it alone can reconcile us to suffering and the deaths of children, it alone can justify them, since we cannot understand them, and we can only make God's will ours. . . . That is the faith, cruel in man's eyes and crucial in God's, that we must ever strive to compass. We must aspire beyond ourselves toward this high and fearful vision. And on that lofty plane all will fall into place, all discords be resolved, and truth flash forth from the dark cloud of seeming injustice.[13]

Thus we are left with the two options Kierkegaard advances: On the one hand we can trust the human perspective and make it ultimate. This, for Panaloux, is tantamount to hating God, and to denying everything. The other alternative, which Panaloux endorses and which Camus concludes is forced upon the Christian, is to accept as good for man what is not comprehended because it contradicts man's highest rational and moral categories.[14]

Panaloux is unambiguous on this point. It is wrong, he argues, for the Christian to say:

> *This* I understand, but *that* I cannot accept. . . . The Christian should yield himself wholly to the divine will even though it passes his understanding. . . . We must go straight to the heart of that which is unacceptable, precisely because it is thus that we are constrained to make our choice.[15]

The "beyond human comprehension" theodicy advanced by Panaloux here has far-reaching implications for the issue of divine racism. Just as the multievidential character of suffering suggests the possibility of a demonic deity, aspects of the theodicy of last resort lead to the same conclusion.

Once appeal is made to a plane beyond human comprehension, we enter an area where X could be non-X; that is, what appears to be malicious and dehumanizing from the human perspective could be consummate justice and love from the divine outlook.[16] And here the concept of a demonic deity or divine racism finds fertile soil.

But another defect logically scars this strategy. The "beyond human comprehension" tactic was introduced to make a place for the ultimate goodness of God in the face of hostile evidence. And to accomplish this, the ultimacy of the human perspective was denied. But to deny the functional ultimacy of man's perspective destroys the very concept this denial was supposed to support. Once we negate the ultimacy of the human outlook, we lay the foundation for the transvaluation of X into non-X; the love of God we were concerned to defend at all costs can be transmuted into its opposite, and we are back again at the very question that initiated the original argument: Is God benevolent? It should be clear that the theodicy of last resort requires a basic continuity between the human and the divine value system. But it is precisely this continuity which is called into question, both by the "beyond human comprehension" strategy and by the fact of suffering itself.

It would appear that the theodicy of last resort has been acceptable only because of its question-begging starting point: the intrinsic benevolence of God. The attitude of complete trust and confidence in God and His promises, that "though He slay me yet I will trust Him" spirit, makes sense only to the degree that God's intrinsic and universal benevolence is granted. It has been my concern to challenge this interpretation of the divine nature.

It is now necessary to highlight certain aspects of the theodicy of last resort in Camus's analysis, and in this way indicate where my viewpoint diverges from his. Camus tends to interpret faith as a leap into the quicksand of blind and unsupported belief; faith for him is to act in a manner that is contrary to the evidence. He suggests that the Christian chooses to act *as if*, "appearances notwithstanding, all trials, however cruel, work together for good to the Christian. And . . . what the Christian should also seek in his hour of trial is to discern that good, in what it consisted and how best he could turn it to account."[17] The Christian, in sum, resolves to regard ultimate reality, counterevidence notwithstanding, as good and supportive of man's true good.

My view of faith is different. We must allow for the possibility that behind the leap of faith is the vigorous push of a concrete but private experience, one that is not visible to the general public. I do not in any way wish to deny the presence or vitality of this type of self-authenticating experience. In fact, to do so would undermine my own position. I insist only upon the admission that the experience is multievidential. I demand only that the individual be willing to acknowledge that he intervenes at some point as the valuator of its significance and the interpreter of its meaning. I shall have more to say on this topic subsequently.

Camus's position forces another questionable conclusion: The real effect of his argument is to compel a choosing of sides that for him are mutually exclusive. In the face of the undeserved suffering of the innocent, one must choose between humanism and theism. The former, to use Panaloux's description, hates God, and gives ultimacy to the human perspective. The latter loves God, and denies ultimacy to the human viewpoint.

I question whether the problem of suffering forces a parting of the way, into camps of theism and humanism, particularly if they are defined as opposites. The investigation of this issue led me to the framing of the position of humanocentric theism. I contend that it is neither a demonstrative theodicy nor a theodicy of last resort. It thus belies the exclusive character of these alternatives; it also opposes the view that humanism and theism are theologically incompatible. In Part III I will show that humanocentric theism and secular humanism are near kin.

Theodicy and Quietism

Most of Camus's interpreters conclude that the second sermon terminates his analysis of suffering and his criticism of Christian theodicy. But this is to miss the focal point of his argument. The two sermons provide the background discussion of suffering which is necessary for the decisive turn in his argument. His main criticism of Christian theodicy is encapsuled in the cryptic and pregnant question, Should a priest consult a doctor? Packed into this question is the fundamental issue of the relation of theodicy and quietism. What is man's proper response to the suffering he himself encounters and that which afflicts his neighbor? Having adopted a theodicy, is one committed, under the guillotine of inconsistency, to accept suffering without rebellion? Is one required to endure whatever suffering impinges? How does one justify corrective actions against suffering? Can this justification emerge from the traditional theodicies of Christian thought? Must one assign a particular quality to suffering as a precondition for its elimination or correction? Can this quality be established in the framework of the traditional Christian theodicies?

I get the strong impression that Camus wants to argue that the theodicy of last resort pushes the issue of quietism to the forefront. In fact the connection between the theodicy of the second sermon and quietism is explicitly established in the novel before the second sermon is delivered. Panaloux informs us that he is working on a pamphlet, which bears the title *Is a Priest Justified in Consulting a Doctor?*[18] and that a forthcoming sermon, the second, would express his considered opinion on the question.

The question, however, is not explicitly broached in the sermon, but some of his explicit statements reveal that Panaloux finds nothing inappropriate about a priest consulting a doctor:

There was no question of not taking precautions or failing to comply with the orders wisely promulgated for the public weal in the disorders of a pestilence. Nor should we listen to certain moralists who told us to sink on our knees and give up the struggle. No, we should go forward, groping our way through the darkness, stumbling, perhaps, at times, and try to do what good lies in our power. As for the rest, we must hold fast, trusting in the divine goodness, even as to the deaths of little children, and not seeking personal respite.[19]

But other comments of Camus, placed in the mouth of another priest, suggest that the theological security of the second sermon is unsure: "In his opinion, the sermon had displayed more uneasiness than real power, and at Panaloux's age a priest had no reason to feel uneasy." This interpretation is strengthened when it is further suggested that the forthcoming pamphlet "might well be refused the imprimatur."[20] And when Panaloux later becomes ill with plague-like symptoms, his own behavior strongly suggests that the issue of theodicy and quietism was only temporarily resolved by the logic of his second sermon.

What is the argument that underlies the charge of quietism? To construct it we must begin with the theodicy of the first sermon, in which the plague is said to be a form of deserved punishment. It is emphasized that the plague first appears in the biblical record to strike down God's enemies, thus proving that God has utilized suffering as a form of punishment. On this basis, then, one can argue that for any instance of suffering, we must allow that it may be merited punishment. But if the suffering is deserved punishment, it should be endured without a dodge, particularly if we affirm Panaloux's principle, "Since it is God's will, we, too, should will it."[21] Otherwise the sufferer enlarges his guilt, for he is now involved in disobedience.

Obviously, any attempt to eliminate or reduce suffering, by that very act, is a direct challenge to the appropriateness of that suffering. Why would one attack suffering if he were not assailing its duration, its severity, etc.? To repeat an earlier conclusion: the precondition for any corrective approach to suffering is the prior definition of that suffering as evil, or negative. Thus a theodicy of deserved punishment thwarts the precondition for the development of a corrective approach to suffering, for to move against suffering is certainly to discredit the claim that it is deserved.

The net effect of a theodicy of deserved punishment, then, is to maintain the status quo. Accordingly, the charge of quietism is justified. And whether the suffering is my own or my neighbor's, the conclusion is the same: the only way to avoid the consequence of quietism is to challenge frontally the initial premise. It must be demonstrated that the suffering is not deserved punishment.

Having shown that deserved punishment is a possible interpretation of suffering and that a theodicy of deserved punishment involves quietism, we have arrived at the position where we can demand the following: the Christian who wants to eliminate suffering or reduce it, the Christian who wants to heal the sick, must confirm that the suffering at issue is not deserved punishment. Such a demonstration, I conclude, is exceedingly difficult to formulate. It is already clear that an inspection of the suffering itself is not a sufficient basis for determining its specific quality or purpose. Thus, to show that deserved punishment is not the case, one must describe what is the case; one must indicate the status, purpose, and place of suffering in God's scheme of things. In the final analysis, we are required to psychoanalyze God or affirm an essential and unambiguous knowledge of His will and purpose. But it is precisely this knowledge—and here the conclusion of the second sermon is crucial—that a theodicy of last resort cannot legitimately supply. God's ways and purpose remain enveloped in mystery and obscurity.

Critics may regard the demand for an unambiguous response as an unfair requirement. I can only note that the interpretation of deserved punishment and its specter of quietism remain as long as the lingering ambiguity endures. One must also recognize that the theodicy of last resort does not actually show that suffering is not deserved punishment. One must also note that there is twofold risk attending failure to refute the theodicy of deserved punishment. By taking the offensive against suffering, we risk being disobedient to God. But we also run the risk of evading the full weight of His judgment and the necessary compensation for our wrongdoings. In short it appears that if the question of merited punishment is not decisively resolved, one is pushed psychologically, if not logically, toward quietism.

Panaloux's own case illustrates the point well. He becomes ill with plague-like symptoms a few days after the delivery of the second sermon. Though his housekeeper urges him to call the doctor, he refuses on the grounds, incomprehensible to her, that it is against his principle. Later, however, he asks to be taken to the hospital in order to comply with the regulations. And "there he submitted passively to the treatment given him, all the while clutching his crucifix." The final notation on his hospital record, "doubtful case,"[22] is intended to convey more than the uncertainty that the plague caused his death. Rather, I think Camus is asking if Panaloux, in fact, followed his principle consistently. In this way Camus also raises the unsettling question, can the theodicy of last resort be the ground for a consistent life style; is it an existential possibility; or is it like skepticism—a position that can be verbalized but contradicts itself once it is put into practice?

Consider the dilemma facing Panaloux. If he interprets conformity to God's will to mean total avoidance of medical aid—and this must be allowed in the context of suffering as deserved punishment—his actions undercut the health regulations designed to curtail the dreaded disease. At this point he becomes guilty of treating his neighbor improperly. In other words, to fulfill the injunction to love his neighbor, he is required to execute the very acts that indicate he has refuted, without sufficient grounds, the interpretation of suffering as deserved punishment.

Dubious Theological Responses to Quietism

If the previous analysis is sound, a viable theodicy for black theology must avoid the strait jacket of quietism. Thus it is necessary to consider more adequate solutions to Panaloux's dilemma. The positions of humanocentric theism and secular humanism developed, for me, as the most appropriate theological response to quietism. In this search we considered and rejected several viewpoints that merit discussion here.

Quietism is avoided if we simply regard *all* suffering as something to be eliminated. There is ample biblical and theological justification for this option, so it is not as farfetched as it may first appear: the pre-Fall state of man as well as his eschatological, or heavenly, situation are alleged to be free from suffering. Thus the starting point and terminus of human destiny exclude suffering. Moreover, if we emphasize a suggested interpretation of Genesis that sees suffering and/or death as the result of man's sin, the elimination of suffering is again dictated. The work of Jesus, as depicted in Luke 4: 18–19, also seems to advance the same goal. And finally, if we compare the biblical descriptions of the New Age and the Kingdom of God with what each replaces, the point is clear.

The defect of this formula, however, soon emerges. Most acute is the problem of the continued suffering of man, especially that of an oppressed group. Suffering that extends over long periods suggests that God has been a quietist, in contradiction to the necessities of the theory, or else one is pushed toward the unattractive choice of an eschatological theodicy.

To make the same point in another way: If one considers this elimination theory of suffering in the light of the reduction of suffering for one group, i.e. the oppressors, but the continued disproportionate suffering of the oppressed, the issue of God's partiality quickly surfaces. From the black perspective the issue of divine racism would be raised.

If, however, one rejects the elimination theory, he is saddled with a monumental theological task. He is required to provide a criterion to differentiate between sufferings that should be ruthlessly attacked and those that should be patiently endured. The implementation of this requirement in my initial research pushed me in the direction of humanism, though later investigations revealed that similar conclusions were possible from the theistic side, i.e. humanocentric theism. The following argument helps to explain the reason for this shift in theological orientation.

We recall that the issue of quietism arose in part because of inability to determine the status and quality of suffering from God's outlook. This problem, however, can be resolved, and the noose of quietism slipped, if the definition of the quality of suffering rests upon man's valuation. The only requirement for taking the offensive against suffering is man's designation of that suffering as oppressive. How God would regard it is not decisive.

I insist that human valuation is in fact functionally ultimate: man of necessity is the supreme arbiter of values for man. Though we may argue that our values have God or some extrahuman agency as their source, we, in the final analysis, determine their value by judging, for instance, the *source* of the value. The same point can be made about the category of revelation.

Martin Buber's analysis of Kierkegaard's concept of the "teleological suspension of the ethical" illustrates the point. To comprehend Buber's criticism we must recall the Genesis story of God's command to Abraham to slay Isaac.

> The problematics of the decision of faith is preceded by the problematics of the hearing itself. Who is it whose voice one hears? For Kierkegaard it is self-evident because of the Christian tradition in which he grew up that he who demands [Isaac's] sacrifice is none other than God. But, for the Bible, at least for the Old Testament, it is not without further question self-evident. Indeed, a

certain instigation to a forbidden act is even ascribed in one place to God and in another to Satan. . . . Thus the question of questions which takes precedence over every other is: Are you really addressed by the Absolute or by one of His apes?[23]

Given the impossibility of demonstrating that the voice is God's and not Moloch's—and it must be remembered that Moloch demanded human sacrifice and accordingly the command to sacrifice Isaac is more compatible with His demands than Yahweh's—the ultimate valuator can only be Abraham, which is to say, man. Abraham makes the final decision regarding the source of the command. If he concludes that the voice is God's, he is, at the same time, affirming that the command is good and ought to be obeyed. If, however, he concludes that the voice is Moloch's, the command is evil and must be rejected. But only Abraham can make this decisive ruling.

Another option for handling quietism is to sever any connection between God's sovereignty and the crimes of human history. This alternative demands that we look afresh at God's sovereignty as it relates to human history. This development led us finally to emphasize human history as the product of human actions, and more important, the product of human power relations. Later we will see both elements—man as the ultimate valuator of values and man as the ultimate actor in history—as essential tenets of secular humanism and humanocentric theism.

IV

DIVINE RACISM AND
THEOLOGICAL METHOD

The Method of Internal Criticism

Part II critically analyzes the treatment of black suffering in the available black theologies, and I present that analysis as primarily an exercise in internal criticism. Such an approach obliges me to demonstrate two essential propositions: (1) The key elements of the critical apparatus used to analyze the black theologians are present either explicitly or implicitly in the black theologians' own materials. (2) Their own presuppositions and conclusions make the question "Is God a white racist?" and its refutation the necessary point of departure for the construction of their respective systems.

The argument thus far, however, has appealed principally to materials independent of the black theologians themselves; many non-black theologians have used the same data and expressed a different theological orientation. For these reasons, the previous argument may appear to violate the canons of internal criticism. To justify the foregoing direction of the argument and the use of materials, it is necessary to say that two separate and independent arguments establish the cen-

trality of theodicy and the issue of divine racism for black
theology. And either argument is sufficient to prove my thesis.
The argument in Chapter V demonstrates the thesis by using
the bricks and mortar the black theologians employ to construct their systems. The previous argument, however, has
attempted to make the same case by formulating some general principles that apply to both black and non-black
theologies.

But the foregoing argument, at the same time, can be considered as an aspect of the over-all internal criticism, and this
will become clear when the general principles already enun-
ciated are shown to be implicit in the black theologies to be
examined.

It has been argued, for instance, that the multievidentiality
of suffering, when connected with ethnic suffering, raises the
issue of divine racism, allowing, of course, for the black
theologians' own presupposition of Western monotheism and
God's activity in and sovereignty over human history. In
short, the issue of divine racism becomes central once black
suffering is made central. If the argument here is sound,
then I can show eventually that a focus on black suffering
obliges black theologians to consider the issue of divine racism. It has also been argued that to regard one's system as a
theology of liberation—a general conclusion of each black
theologian—is to push suffering to the center of the theological
discussion. Does not liberation mean liberation from oppression or its near kin? And oppression as defined by the black
theologians invariably involves excessive suffering as its core.
In sum, the centrality of black suffering can be extracted
from the black theologians' stated purpose—to formulate a
theology of liberation.

The Threshold Question

The method of internal criticism can be clarified by intro-
ducing the concept of a threshold issue or question. There
are certain unavoidable questions and issues that confront

the philosopher or theologian when he begins his systematic work. This question cannot be evaded, because the theologian's program and the superstructure of his system presuppose an answer to it. Ethics, to take an obvious example, cannot proceed without first refuting the challenge of ethical nihilism, which denies the very possibility of the enterprise of ethics. Similarly a theology is committed to a discussion of the existence and nature of God, and this entails some implicit or explicit response to the opposing view of atheism or humanism. A theologian who advances his system as Christian cannot evade the issue of Christology. An adequate refutation of the opposing position must be given—or else it must be admitted that a refutation is not possible, thus committing oneself to a confessional or assumptive foundation for one's system. If this is not done, the remainder of the system is without adequate support, for clearly it would be built upon a question-begging foundation.

That the threshold question or issue basically controls the theological enterprise can be easily shown. Its answer commits the theologian to a certain methodology, a particular set of categories, or a specific position on the theological spectrum, and these features control and guide the theologian's task. This initial "taking of a position," which the threshold question compels, gives the remainder of the system a particular shape. And clearly any discontinuity between the answer to the threshold issue and the system's superstructure leads to an internal contradiction.

Many, if not most, theological works begin at a point well beyond the threshold issue, and this issue, for many texts, legitimately falls outside the scope of concern. Nonetheless, even in such instances, the theologian should be conscious of the omission and its possible connection with his present venture. If he is prudent and careful, his work will be consistent with the position he would have taken relative to the threshold issue—if it had in fact been dealt with. And if the theologian is not conscious of the omission, then it is the task of his critics to appraise his work in the light of the threshold issue that it invariably presupposes.

With this understanding, it should now be clear that I have been engaged in a discussion of the threshold issue for black theology.

Divine Racism and the Method of Counterevidence

It is now possible to call attention to some of the methodological implications of the previous discussion, and this is necessary since they involve part of the critical apparatus of our investigation.

I gather from the inverted interpretation of traditional theological categories, e.g. Golgotha as an example of divine misanthropy, this conclusion: theology must utilize the method of counterevidence. The same conclusion is forced by the multievidential quality of phenomena.

This method, as the name suggests, focuses upon evidence contrary to the position the theologian wishes to defend. The materials negating the theologian's own position are precisely those which must be afforded the most careful, deliberate, and sympathetic consideration. Given the method of counterevidence, the theologian must furnish a framework capable of accommodating the materials that contradict his own. Panaloux, for instance, was persuaded to abandon the theodicy of deserved punishment, because it could not assimilate the scandal event, the death of the innocent child.[1]

Frederick Sontag's apologia for theism clarifies the method even more. He describes his method as "the argument from the existence of the devil," that is, "the negative and destructive forces which are loose in the world."[2] He attempts to account for God's existence and construct a concept of His nature from the complex of experiences, notably human suffering, that have been the foundation for traditional atheism. Thus the materials of atheism become the primary if not the exclusive blocks for Sontag's statement of theism. As he himself describes the method:

The aim is . . . to see if we can form a possible concept
of God from the very sources of the argument against
him. . . . Can we learn anything new about God by
examining the origins of the denial of his existence?
This is an attempt at a new *via negativa.* . . . If any
concept of God is incapable of accounting for the existence of the factors that argue against him, it cannot
really describe God, since the forces leading toward
atheism are very real and would have to be created
willingly and knowingly by any God worthy of his name.
. . . Two alternatives are always open to us. . . . We
may form a positive concept of God from his acknowledged perfections (e.g., Goodness) as these are present
in the world, and then work hard to give the devil the
reality due to him; or we may simply start with the devil
. . . from the accumulated negative elements. . . . This
is the argument from the existence of the devil, but
whether it will yield two Gods or only one it is impossible to know in advance.[3]

Sontag's description of the argument from "the accumulated negative elements" corresponds to the method of
counterevidence. I question whether the other approach he permits, beginning with a "positive concept of God," is valid.
The argument from God's "acknowledged perfections" appears to beg the question. Can we start, for instance, with
the alleged goodness of God and then try to accommodate
the accumulated negative elements without begging the question? Until the alleged negative elements are appropriately
reconciled with the alleged benevolence of God, His goodness
remains an open question.

What I wish to insist upon is the recognition of the multievidential quality of the materials themselves and the necessity of trying to let the "positive" and "negative" labels be
conclusions reached about the experiences in question—not
presuppositions brought to the analysis of these experiences.
I do not insist that one must *begin* with an investigation of

the counterevidential materials, but only that the completed framework accommodate them.

The importance of the counterevidence approach for theodicy cannot be overemphasized. Indeed I am tempted to argue that the issue of divine racism emerges only to the degree that this approach is adopted. Traditionally the theologian has not utilized this model. Rather than beginning with an analysis of "evil," rather than considering the multievidentiality of the "positive" elements, he has started his work in theodicy with a specific and assumed concept of God. Thus the view that God is one, creator, benevolent, etc. is the presupposed framework into which the "evil" is forced.

This traditional approach has a dual effect: It obviously eliminates by definition other explanations of suffering and evil, for example dualism, a demonic deity, and the like. It precludes at the outset other resolutions that can consistently account for human suffering and oppression and that, too, are grounded in human experience. The accumulated effect of this traditional approach is to create a theological climate hostile to the consideration of categories such as divine racism. Such can emerge only after the original concept of God has been seriously challenged, and to accomplish this appears to necessitate the counterevidence approach.

If, however, one starts with the event of suffering—I am presupposing its multievidentiality here—rather than the prejudiced concept in the traditional approach, different methodological requirements are demanded. One is required to construct a doctrine of God that can come to terms with the suffering at issue. In this way the counterevidence method has the crucial effect of placing rival interpretations, at the outset, on equal footing. "God is a soul brother" and "God is a white racist" possess equal interpretive probability. The rival interpretations of divine benevolence and divine malevolence enjoy coequal probability. In short, the method of theologizing by reference to the counterevidence allows the full weight of the "negative" evidence to bear in a telling way on the theological discussion.

Gnosiological Conversion: the Initial Task of Black Theology

The intimate connection between theodicy and oppression has forcible implications for the black theologian's method and purpose. I conclude that the initial task of the black theologian is to liberate the black mind from the destructive ideas and submissive attitudes that checkmate any movement toward authentic emancipation. It is to effect what I term the gnosiological conversion of the black psyche.

Conversion here means the fundamental reconstruction and reorientation of the individual's present world view and life style. It involves a conscious renunciation of one's present position as wrong, and it seeks to replace the old beliefs with a more realistic picture of man and reality, and the anachronistic attitudes and actions with those capable of producing the ideal humanity. Gnosiological here means the shift is primarily one of concepts and beliefs; it relates to one "knowledge." Thus the object of the theologian's analysis should be what his black sisters and brothers believe to be true about themselves and the universe of nature and society, for it is this knowledge that regulates their actions. Gnosiological conversion, in the black context, reduces to the "deniggerification" of blacks.

The task of gnosiological conversion breaks down into more concrete tasks. First, the ideas and concepts that undergird oppression must be clearly isolated and quarantined, both from the side of the oppressor's world view and from that of the oppressed's. I insist that the first item to be investigated is the oppressor's and the oppressed's concept of theodicy; most often this will involve demolishing the theodicies currently in vogue.

Camus and Sartre provide a helpful clue for accomplishing this task. Their approach involves a variant of the *reductio ad absurdum* argument. That is, I overturn my opponent's position by showing that it embraces a conclusion that is unreasonable or that it is unable to refute a position that is ridiculous or improbable. With this understanding, my use of the category of divine racism can be regarded as an *ad absurdum* argument. My concern is not to establish the truth of the charge of divine racism. Rather, my intent is to demonstrate that the normative frameworks of the black theologians are questionable, because they raise the issue of divine racism and, once raised, cannot effectively refute the charge with their present theological resources. In this sense, divine racism is a useful polemical tool, disregarding for the moment its truth value.

Another aspect of the black theologian's method is pinpointed when we consider additional features of oppression: the oppressor justifies his own exalted status and the appalling misery of the oppressed through an appeal to some extrahuman ground. Appeal, for example, is made to God's will, to the biological attributes of the oppressor relative to the oppressed, to some natural law as the basis for the difference in status or accomplishment, etc. This is to say, in effect, that extrahuman agencies or processes are ultimately responsible for the abnormalities and inequities of human history. It makes, as we have seen, God the ultimate racist. The appeal to extrahuman sanctions also effectively releases the oppressor from any sense of responsibility and guilt for the oppressed's suffering. Both his state and that of the oppressed are the natural, the given, that which is supported by ultimate reality. Obviously, as Panaloux and others suggest, rebellion here is almost unthinkable, for it would involve challenging ultimate reality.

A theology of liberation must provide persuasive grounds for removing the sanctity and hallowed status from those segments of the culture it seeks to reform. The black theologians to be examined desanctify the roots of oppression by invoking the divine activity, purpose, or revelation, for example—the politics of God. I, however, find it preferable to utilize the principle of the functional ultimacy of man to achieve the same goal.

PART II

✱✱✱✱✱✱✱✱✱✱✱✱✱

Black Suffering and Black Theology:
An Internal Critique

V

DIVINE RACISM: THE UNACKNOWLEDGED THRESHOLD ISSUE FOR BLACK THEOLOGY

This chapter purports to show that the issue of divine racism has been illegitimately ignored by the current black theologians. I say "illegitimately" because the question has been avoided only by disregarding concrete and explicit features of their own thought. Since specific conclusions advanced by the black theologians are meaningful and valid only if they provide a convincing refutation of the charge of divine racism, the absence of an analysis and denial of the question "Is God a white racist?" constitutes a curious inconsistency and removes the necessary support the superstructure of their respective systems requires. I will show specifically that the issue of divine racism is implicit in the following propositions affirmed by the black theologians: black theology is a theology of liberation; the politics of God and blacks as God's chosen people are central themes in black theology; and black theology is committed to a total and comprehensive examination of the Christian tradition.

Divine Racism: Explicit and Implicit

The same argument cannot be used to demonstrate that the issue of divine racism is central for each black theologian. For most, it is necessary to proceed by way of inference, showing that an explicit concept, conclusion, or methodological position acknowledged by the black theologian presupposes the question of divine racism or its refutation. However, for one theologian, James Cone, the route of logical inference is not required, for the concept is explicitly asserted in a way that reveals its centrality. Cone declares: "Either God is identified with the oppressed to the point that their experience becomes his, or he is a god of racism."[1] And to remove all doubt regarding the meaning of "identification," he claims in a similar vein, "Black theology refuses to accept a God who is not identified totally with the goals of the black community. If God is not for us and against white people, then he is a murderer, and we had better kill him. The task of black theology is to kill Gods who do not belong to the black community."[2]

These statements clearly indicate that Cone is not only aware of the issue of divine racism, but even more important, he regards it as an unavoidable issue for black theology. Note that his analysis establishes two opposing options, which define the arena for black theological discussion and construction. There is the option of "a God of racism," one who is *against* or *indifferent to* black liberation. The second option is the logical and theological opposite: a God *for* black liberation. By defining the task of black theology as destroying Gods who are not for black liberation, Cone is maintaining that the black theologian must effectively refute the position of divine racism. In fact he appears to claim that the black theologian can defend the position that God is for black liberation, only by refuting the charge that He is a god of racism. His words also convey the meaning that this refutation is the crucial part of the black theologian's task. If the analysis of Cone here is correct, then his own definition of the purpose of black theology creates the exact critical apparatus and the rules of the game I will use to criticize his system.

It is not difficult to show that the theodicy issue is also central for the remaining black theologians, and these factors further establish its centrality for Cone. The starting point for this demonstration is the conclusion already established: suffering introduces the theodicy question. Thus the general issue of theodicy and the particular issue of divine racism are central because of the status the black theologians assign to black suffering. Theodicy and divine racism are controlling issues because black oppression and suffering are made the starting point for theological analysis.

It can now be established that black suffering is either explicitly or implicitly central for the contemporary black theologians. Here is an explicit reference from the theology of James Cone: "The point of departure for black theology is the question, How do we dare speak of God in a suffering world . . . in which blacks are humiliated because they are black? This question . . . occupies the central place in our theological perspective."[3]

A similar emphasis is present in J. Deotis Roberts' discussion of "The Black Man's God."

> I am taking the position that the problem of God presents itself to blacks in terms, not of the existence of God, but rather in terms of the moral attributes of God. . . . The Christian understanding of God must develop out of the black presence in a white racist society, and out of an experience of oppression endured for almost four centuries.[4]

What is not always explicit in the language of black theology may often lie implicit. For example, once "black liberation" is established as the primary goal or the rationale for black theology, black suffering becomes its necessary starting point. "Liberation" as defined by the black theologians means nothing if it does not mean release from the

suffering that lies at the heart of oppression. To define liberation as the *summum bonum,* the highest good for blacks, is,
at the same time, to make that suffering which is the core of
oppression the essential ingredient of the *summum malum,*
the ultimate evil.

Each of the black theologians regards his position as a
theology of liberation, and this motif is usually proclaimed
in the title of the work: *A Black Theology of Liberation,
Liberation and Reconciliation: A Black Theology.* Even
where "liberation" is absent from the title, it is soon discovered
to be the black theologian's principal focus.

What is less obvious is that the issue of divine racism becomes an unavoidable issue in the context of any "black
theology of liberation." To undertake the construction of a
black theology of liberation requires the prior conclusion
that black suffering is oppressive or negative. God disapproves
of it; He does not demand that blacks should endure it. But
suffering is multievidential;[5] it can express a relation of divine favor or disfavor. Consequently, the possibility of divine
disfavor cannot be avoided.

By virtue of his task, the black theologian of liberation is
committed to the view that black oppression is not evidence
of divine disfavor. Accordingly, he is required to show—if he
is to avoid the indictment of begging the question—that the
general class of divine disfavor, of which divine racism is a
subclass, does not accurately describe the black situation.

Other segments of the black theologian's thought force
the issue of divine racism. It has already been established
that ethnic suffering raises the question of divine racism.
Accordingly it is necessary only to demonstrate that the black
theologians describe black suffering as a variety of ethnic
suffering. It will become clear that each affirms that black
suffering is maldistributed, enormous, dehumanizing, and
transgenerational. At this juncture, however, it is sufficient
to note that to define the black situation as *oppressive* is
actually to affirm the essentials of ethnic suffering; and the
definition of the black situation as oppressive, we have seen,

is the consequence of the black theologian's own definition of his task as a theology of liberation.

The Politics of God, and Blacks as God's Chosen People

There are other determining factors that oblige the black theologian to resolve the issue of divine racism at the outset of his theological construction, and these are factors common to his basic position. Each black theologian affirms the doctrine of the politics of God as an essential plank. Man must decide where God is working for human liberation in our midst and join Him in the struggle. The following statement from Cone is representative of this viewpoint: "Black theology merely tries to discern the activity of the Holy One as he effects his purpose in the liberation of man from the forces of oppression. We must make decisions about where God is at work so we can join him in his fight against evil."[6]

But given ethnic suffering and the multievidentiality of suffering, certain restrictions are placed on the theological employment of the politics of God. Without the prior refutation of the charge of divine racism, the black theologian begs the question if he affirms the politics of God. It goes without saying that Cone and others advocate joining God because they presuppose that He is on the side of blacks. This is to say that where God is active in human affairs He is engaged for the (a) good of (b) blacks—if not all of mankind. But ethnic suffering and the multievidentiality of suffering call both (a) and (b) into question. The excessive amount of black suffering and its enormity, both of which are admitted by calling the black situation oppressive, make it risky if not foolhardy to affirm that God is at work for the liberation of blacks. Must not the black theologian first explain how their plight came about in the first place in the face of God's alleged activity in their behalf? In sum, it is not possible to make the politics of God the second floor of the edifice of black theology without a foundational theodicy that decisively answers the charge of divine racism. The politics of

God presupposes that God is not a white racist, without establishing it.

Much the same argument can be made regarding another favorite motif of black theology: blacks as God's "chosen people." To regard blacks as God's elect involves the prior conclusion that God is favorably inclined toward them. But this claim can be made only if the opposite relation, divine disfavor, has been effectively eliminated. And this, again, demands the refutation of divine racism as logically prior to any proposition about divine favor.

Divine Racism and a *de Novo* Theology

The precondition for constructing a black theology is the conviction that an unacknowledged white theology, a theology of racism and oppression, dominates the field. Black theology, then, by definition is committed to a theological development not only beyond this white theology but in conscious and fundamental opposition to it. My purpose now is to show that this understanding of black theology requires a *de novo* approach to theologizing and that within this context the issue of divine racism cannot be avoided.

The black theologians assign primacy to the black experience as the theological norm. It is argued, for instance, that theological reflection must begin with the questions and issues that are pressing upon the black mind and heart. In this way, the black experience determines the theological agenda; it selects the appropriate theological issues, and ranks them. Moreover, the answers must not only harmonize with the black experience, they must also hasten the actualization of the aspirations incarnate in the black hope.

Again, the black experience passes final judgment upon the functional and dysfunctional quality of the entire theological tradition. A theological concept is functional if and only if it advances black liberation or liberation-reconciliation. As Cone concludes, "The legitimacy of any language, religious or otherwise, is determined by its usability in the struggle for liberation."[7]

On the basis of the foregoing analysis—and here we arrive at the crucial point for the argument—the black theologian is committed to a total examination of the theological tradition. Once it is concluded that Christianity is infected with "Whitianity," once it is granted that a racist doctrine of the tradition has been perpetuated, the tradition must be scrutinized in the most radical and comprehensive manner. Like the rotten apples in the barrel of good apples, nothing prior to the examination can be regarded as sacrosanct for black theology—be it God, Jesus, or the Bible. Each and every category must be painstakingly inspected, and if it is found to be infected with the virus of racism or oppression, it must be cast aside.

The same point can be made from another perspective: Once the black theologian is convinced that a racist variety of Christian faith has continued, he must proceed, as it were, *de novo,* placing the entire tradition under a rigid theological ban. And this ban can be lifted only when each part proves its orthodoxy by showing its racist quotient to be minimal.

I question whether the black theologians have recognized the sweeping consequences of their presuppositions here. I also take the position that their appraisal has not been sufficiently comprehensive and radical. From my vantage point I see a fatal residue of the oppressor's world view in some of their theistic premises, in particular the intrinsic goodness of God. One of the compelling reasons for raising the issue of divine racism is to force a discussion of traditional concepts of God as possible props for oppression.

The major point can now be made: From a *de novo* perspective, the rival claims, God is a white racist and God is a soul brother, stand on equal footing. Accordingly, the black theologian cannot avoid the issue of divine racism. In fact it can be argued that he contradicts himself methodologically if he emphasizes black suffering and calls for a comprehensive scrutiny of the tradition but fails to raise the question of divine racism.

The presuppositions of the black theologians, in summary, force the conclusion that the foundation for their systems must be a theodicy that effectively rebuts the charge that God is a white racist. Whether they provide the requisite rebuttal can only be determined by critical inspection of their thought, and it is to this task that the remaining chapters in Part II are devoted.

I would insist at the outset of that examination that the black theologian cannot simply assume the falsity of the charge. His own norm makes this plain. Black suffering must be analyzed from an existential and not an abstract or theoretical perspective. The question of divine racism emerges because of the blood and guts of black suffering. The black theologian, accordingly, must utilize evidential materials drawn from the actual black experience, past, present—and if he dares—the future. What is to be rejected are mere rational and theoretical formulations that are not substantiated by the actual history of blacks. In this connection I will contend that the liberation of non-blacks, e.g. the Jews in the Exodus account, can never count decisively against the charge that God is a white racist.

VI

JOSEPH WASHINGTON: BLACKS
AS GOD'S SUFFERING SERVANT

There are several sound reasons to make the thought of
Joseph Washington the point of departure for a discussion
of black suffering in contemporary black theology. His treatment dramatically illustrates the specific concept of God that
introduces the concept of divine racism. Given his description of God's sovereignty over human history and His activity
within it, God's malice for blacks seems the most probable
explanation of black suffering. The theology of suffering that
informs his major work, *The Politics of God,* can easily be
read as an elaborate master plan for divine racism.[1] His
thought also illustrates the theological tightrope the black
theologian must walk when he tries to accommodate ethnic
suffering within traditional theological patterns, especially
some time-honored biblical models. My criticism will focus
on two places where Washington is significantly vulnerable:
his deficient refutation of the theodicy of deserved punishment and his inadvisable classification of blacks as a contemporary suffering servant.

Since Washington's theodicy is an elaboration of the theodicy of vicarious suffering, the criticism here constitutes a

general critique of this central model of biblical theodicy. The criticism of Washington, with only slight modification, is also applicable to any black theologian who adopts the theodicy of vicarious suffering, including Martin L. King, for example.[2]

The Theodicy of the Suffering Servant / Chosen People

Washington's theodicy is reducible to the claim that blacks are God's contemporary suffering servant. Indeed he argues that the doctrine of vicarious suffering is the only biblical model that can accommodate the black experience in America. "As a result of this suffering by a whole people for four centuries and placed in the perspective of the Bible, we contend . . . that the Negro cannot be understood or understand himself except as another 'chosen people.' "[3]

Washington's theodicy, joined to the issue of divine racism, results in the following syllogism:

> If blacks are the suffering servant / chosen people, the charge of divine racism is disproved.
> Blacks are the suffering servant / chosen people.
> Therefore the charge of divine racism is disproved.

When the logical structure of Washington's theodicy is examined, it is unmistakable that the soundness of his argument requires the demonstration that blacks are in fact the suffering servant. I contend, however, that when the defining features of the suffering servant are clearly exposed and when blacks and their history are appraised in the light of these features, only one conclusion is possible: Washington's classification of blacks as the suffering servant is, as he himself describes white pretensions to the same title, "a mythical hope with precious little relationship to reality."[4]

Washington's demonstration that blacks are the suffering servant completely collapses because he fails to substantiate two essential propositions: (1) He does not identify the requisite exaltation-liberation event, which is indispensable for the biblical model of the suffering servant. (2) He does not refute the claim that black suffering is deserved punishment.

Washington's theological instinct is certainly correct in focusing upon the suffering servant and its theme of vicarious suffering as an attractive explanation of black suffering in particular and ethnic suffering in general. In fact it must be acknowledged at the outset that if blacks are the suffering servant / chosen people, the charge of divine racism has been effectively refuted. In the context of vicarious suffering it is not scandalous for the servant to receive a double portion of the suffering and misery that define the maldistribution and enormity of ethnic suffering. Actually a surplus of suffering above and beyond what is inherent in the human condition is demanded if the biblical model of suffering servant is to apply legitimately. The only feature of ethnic suffering that the theodicy of vicarious suffering cannot accommodate is the non-catastrophic factor; the exaltation-liberation event, which terminates the excess suffering, would appear to contradict the unrelieved agony associated with non-catastrophic suffering.

Mention of the exaltation-liberation event pinpoints the problem facing the black theologian who wants to adopt the suffering-servant paradigm. Not only must the suffering servant suffer, but, equally important, he must be vindicated. His suffering must cease and be replaced by its opposite. J. Deotis Roberts has captured the essence of the biblical pattern when he observes: "The resurrection is the sequel to the cross. Without Easter morning, Good Friday would be Bad Friday, for evil would have the last word."[5]

Consideration must be given, however, to the possibility that Washington wants to regard the exaltation-liberation event as in the future, an eschatological event. But even this option cannot prevent the collapse of his classification. Is it possible to categorize suffering as vicarious prior to the exaltation event? That suffering is vicarious would appear to be a retrospective determination. Washington himself appears to accept this interpretation in the following statement: "That the Israelites were the chosen ones is a declaration of faith made by the interpreters who in historical perspective have asked and found the meaning of the paradoxical and enigmatic life of the Jewish people."[6] What else can be meant by "historical perspective"? But if the retrospective factor is honored, then clearly any appeal to the exaltation-liberation event as a future occurrence is blocked. Until its actual occurrence the classification of blacks as suffering servant is gratuitous, premature, and question-begging.

This criticism is strengthened if it is recognized that a specific feature of the suffering-servant concept has an argumentative or question-begging factor in the context of the issue of divine racism. Essential to the meaning of suffering servant is the claim that suffering is a sign of divine favor. That is to say, one part of its meaning constitutes an implicit "refutation" of the claim that suffering is a sign of disfavor. Thus the net effect of the mere definition of the suffering servant is to exclude by definition all the subclasses of divine disfavor, including divine racism, deserved punishment, etc. Consequently, simply labeling or calling an individual or group "suffering servant" is to refute in advance the charge of divine racism. But this point must be emphasized: the "refutation" is the consequence of the classification, and only that. The real issue, then, is reduced to this question: Has it been substantiated that blacks are in fact the suffering servant? And this involves ultimately, I contend, the determination of the exaltation-liberation event. Until that event can be established, it is clear that to point to the suffering of a group is never sufficient warrant for indexing it as the suffering servant.

To turn to the second proposition Washington fails to substantiate: it is unmistakable that the validity of his position and the accuracy of his classification of blacks as the suffering servant require that he demonstrate that black suffering is not deserved punishment. This demonstration is all the more pressing since Washington confirms that in the past God has employed suffering as a form of deserved punishment. Accordingly, this interpretation of suffering must be considered as a possible interpretation for present and future suffering, including the suffering of blacks. Washington introduces the possibility of deserved punishment to account for the black plight, but only to dismiss it in a most cavalier and untrustworthy fashion. The following passage exhausts his consideration and "refutation" of the theodicy of deserved punishment:

> Historically, the systematic victimization of the African and the American Negro has been accepted as the punishment of the will of God. But this very belief sparks the reality so opposite, the truth of hope; these victims bear the marks of those blessed of God to do his work of love, rejected by men more acceptable to each other but not to God.[7]

At this point, too, Washington's failure to identify the definitive exaltation-liberation event for blacks is fatal to the validity of his argument. It must be recalled that the suffering servant is innocent; his suffering is not deserved punishment. Hence the necessity of showing that black suffering is not deserved punishment—if the classification as suffering servant is to be accurate. But is it not the exaltation-liberation event that proves that his prior suffering was not deserved, that corroborates the innocence of the sufferer? In sum, without the liberation event the interpretation of deserved punishment still stands, and until it is removed, Washington's classification of blacks as the suffering servant clearly begs the question.

God's Responsibility for Black Suffering

Washington's failure to identify the exaltation-liberation event is sufficient to negate his theodicy. Other features of his position, however, are equally questionable, because they lead to the conclusion that blacks are in the hands of a divine racist and are not His agents of salvation. To explain this point it is necessary to examine Washington's description of the role of blacks in God's larger, saving history for mankind. As a preliminary to this argument, several crucial features of the suffering servant / chosen people must be identified. They are its universality, particularity, and duality. As suffering servant, blacks have a universal mission to mankind in general and a particular mission to the inhabitants of America. The universal mission of the black nation can be comprehended by comparing it with the saving function of another chosen people—the Jews. The universal task God assigned to the Jews was to inform the human family that there is one and only one God. The universal mission of blacks is parallel: "To witness to the one humanity of the one God."[8]

Though Washington does not make this point, it is possible to see the black assignment as a continuation of the monotheistic mission of the Jews. In so far as racism calls into question the unity of mankind, God's oneness is also under attack. Thus the monotheisizing of man must await the humanizing of man, the recognition and acceptance of the disparate tribes of man as one humanity.

The questionable features of Washington's view emerge as soon as it is recognized that the universal mission of blacks begins with a particular mission here in America. Their special task in America is to save the white oppressor from the chains of his irreligious white folk religion and to release him from his idolatrous bondage to racism.

In this sense, the black mission in God's saving history has a dual aspect. Like two sides of the same coin, there is an essential interconnection between the universal and particular aspects of its mission, on the one hand, and black liberation on the other. That is, the means by which blacks execute their particular / universal mission is at the same time the avenue to black liberation.[9] Moreover, whether liberation becomes a reality depends upon the successful execution of their universal / particular assignment.

It must also be understood that Washington identifies the suffering servant as a *group*, not a single individual. "God has called a people, not a man, to be His 'suffering servant.'"[10]

Having presented the essential elements of the black mission, it is now possible to show that Washington's position involves the following consequences, which imply that God is a white racist. In fact, when these consequences are considered jointly, one is hard pressed not to conclude that divine racism should be the favored explanation of black suffering. It is my contention—and here I lay out the parameters of the subsequent argument—that Washington's theodicy (a) asserts the *inevitability* of black suffering, (b) appears to assert the *perpetuity* of black suffering, and (c) affirms that both are in conformity with God's will and purpose.

More specifically, when one spells out the fundamentals of his argument that blacks are the suffering servant, that black suffering conforms to God's will and purpose, that "Negroes can only perceive themselves to be afflicted by God,"[11] that the Lord has laid on blacks the iniquity of whites (and this must be allowed if black suffering is vicarious), and if one emphasizes and interprets divine sovereignty as he does, the conclusion seems inevitable: *God is responsible for black suffering.* And this conclusion surely makes it impossible to avoid the question, Is God a white racist?

That his position asserts the inevitability of black suffering is the first point to be demonstrated. In this connection it must be understood that the suffering at issue is maldistributed. One should also note in Washington's view how God's sovereignty and responsibility emerge as the foundation of the suffering to be analyzed. Finally it must also be recalled that black suffering designates the condition of an entire group and not simply selected individuals.

I conclude that black suffering is inevitable in Washington's system because God has chosen a particular way to accomplish the salvation of mankind: through the vicarious suffering of particular groups. The status of blacks as suffering servant "cannot be canceled," he insists, "by refusing to be obedient; God has chosen us [blacks] to use the suffering color of the Negroes whether or not they choose to accept their destiny."[12] Numerous passages make the same point: black suffering is inevitable, because God has chosen them to serve his purpose, which involves suffering—whether they want to or not.

Negroes would not wish to be called—and would actively resist being—the "chosen people" were they consciously to understand and accept the biblical meaning of being chosen by God: inflicted, stricken, grieved, chastised, an offering poured out as "intercession for the transgressors." But just as they have neither known nor accepted it, this is their history. For it is through their experience that the presence of God in all our midst can be affirmed. Through their suffering "we are all healed"—black and white together.[13]

Note Washington's suggestion here that blacks and Jews also would not have chosen to be the suffering servant, precisely because of the suffering involved. But they actually have no choice; they are the suffering servant as the result of God's choice, not their own. There is no hint that they are even consulted on the matter. Blacks cannot choose not to be the suffering servant. They can only choose to be God's "volunteers" or be guilty of resisting the duties involved in the redemptive suffering they are called to bear. And Washington is unequivocal on this point: man does not possess the power to overrule God's decision:

Just as God does not ask our permission to create us, nor provide us with the choice of being born to this man and this woman in that country and that time, so He does not ask for volunteers as His "suffering servant." Were this not the freedom of God which is as different from the freedom of man as . . . God's time from clock time, there would be no religious meaning to "chosen." If it had been up to the Jews, they would have asked God to do them no favors, and the same is true for the Negro. . . . The real difference between being "chosen" by God and choosing to be "suffering servants" is the absence of choice; whites who choose to suffer . . . have an escape hatch which neither Jews nor Negroes enjoy.[14]

Consequently, black suffering is inescapable. Whether blacks choose to be obedient or disobedient, the result is the same.

Hence his conclusion that the Negro must "choose to be what he is, 'suffering servant,' the source of power, or fatalistically acquiesce in suffering. . . ."[15]

Washington's position here calls attention to a crucial problem that is insufficiently examined by the black theologians: *the relation of human and divine freedom.* The question is obviously crucial for the area of theodicy, for it involves, in the final analysis, the determination of the spheres of human responsibility vis-à-vis the divine control, or the places of their coresponsibility. The importance of this issue is underscored when another aspect of inevitability in Washington's position is considered: He concludes that since "Negroes will always be black and objectionable to whites," they can expect only inhuman treatment from whites because of the "inescapability from being black."[16]

But Washington's appeal to white racism as the causal nexus for black suffering creates a crucial problem that he simply ignores. The fact of white racism must be accounted for in the context of God's sovereignty and freedom. Once he allows that the "freedom of man . . . must operate within the freedom of God,"[17] the issue of God's responsibility for white racism immediately surfaces. A similar issue is taken up below in the discussion of Rubenstein's argument that to affirm God's sovereignty as Washington does is to make God responsible for the horror of Auschwitz. Indeed Washington is willing to go all the way and say that black slavery in America is part of God's plan of salvation for mankind. And indeed he must if he is not to contradict his doctrine of divine sovereignty.[18]

The Perpetuity of Black Suffering

Though suffering may be inevitable, it need not be eternal. Washington, however, asserts both the inevitability and the perpetuity of suffering in a rigid fashion that makes the issue of divine racism unavoidable. An aspect of the previous discussion of the suffering-servant model—the necessity of the exaltation-liberation event—illuminates the issue here. If the occurrence of the exaltation-liberation event is necessary to identify the suffering servant, then the perpetuity of suffering contradicts one's status as God's redemptive agent. This is so because the liberation event terminates the excess suffering and thus removes it from the class of the perpetual. In sum, though the inevitability of suffering is compatible with the role of the suffering servant, the perpetuity of suffering is not.

Several elements of his thought imply the ceaseless progression of black suffering. There is the claim that the suffering of blacks will continue until their divinely appointed mission is successfully completed, and this, he allows, may not occur until the end of time, until the *eschaton*. Just as "the continuing chastisement of the Jews may be to the end of time," so "the Negro will receive no reward until all are healed."[19]

Washington's allowance that black suffering *may* endure until eternity provides a possible exit from the charge of perpetuity. I acknowledge this. But other fundamentals of his position suggest that an accurate description of his thought must replace "may" with "will." Note the interesting consequences of his concept of the duality of black suffering: vicarious suffering is the means by which black liberation is effected. Washington accents the point that black suffering will be continued until the mission is *successfully* completed:

> But the mission of the "suffering servant" Negro people also may not end in time. There will be those who prefer their own group not out of free choice but out of a pre-consciousness. As long as there are such men, so long will the Negro be God's "judgment" upon their "sin" and "transgression." Whom God bruises "for our iniquities," the Anglo-Puritan iniquity that "turned everyone to his own way," God will not let go "to see the fruit of the travail of his soul and be satisfied" until "by his stripes we are healed."[20]

Moreover, when one considers what constitutes the successful execution of the black mission, and the nature of that mission, the issue of perpetuity strikes us in a different form: Is the black mission an *impossible mission?* The question is not rhetorical. Indeed Washington's own admission that black suffering may be to the end of time suggests that he, too, recognizes the enormity and, no doubt, the superhuman demands of the task. Again, when Washington's description of the black mission is laid bare, one receives the strong impression that the victorious completion of its task is actually a utopian ideal. Consider, for instance, the following aspects of the black mission: "Freedom and equality with and for all men,"[21] "releasing whites from their blasphemous bondage to whiteness,"[22] a bondage that is "preconscious" and therefore not amenable to "rational persuasion," "to make group differences [not] irrelevant, but enriching for all mankind,"[23] "to expunge the preconscious white folk religion in the socio-cultural fabric,"[24] that is to say, to annihilate *institutional* racism and to remove it from all areas of American life. It is also "to unify mankind through the acceptance of group differences as blessings rather than punishment,"[25] "to restructure human life on the basis of group acceptance of all other groups,"[26] "to create that situation whereby mankind will consciously, not accidentally, voluntarily, not by force, affirm first in principle and then in practice a life of full human oneness."[27] Is this not what Christians call the Kingdom of God? To make black liberation and the cessation of black suffering hinge upon the actualization of the Kingdom is most assuredly to insure the uninterrupted suffering of blacks until the eschaton.

One is also compelled to ask why Washington concludes that the suffering of blacks will succeed where reason has failed in rehabilitating white religion. Surely he is not endorsing the discredited view of Gandhi[28] (reaffirmed by Martin L. King) that the suffering of the innocent will cause the oppressor to cease his oppression! On the other hand he points to "the grace which follows from the Eternal's purpose" as the source of "inexhaustible courage"[29] and power. This approach is in keeping with his emphatic doctrine of divine sovereignty.

This interpretation is also in line with his claim that the black mission will be successful, and thus effect black liberation, only if we accept and conform to God's method of salvation: vicarious suffering.

But this argument suffers from several defects: First, it requires that Washington substantiate the very proposition the previous analysis has shown to be absent, which is that blacks are the chosen people. Further, without the substantiation that black suffering is a sign of divine favor, any appeal to God as the ultimate guarantor of the black mission's success is to assume what must be proved. If God demands black suffering up to the eschaton, why not beyond it as well?

The same point can be put in another way: One can easily infer from Washington's work the notion of a demonic God. Consider the idea that God has saddled blacks with an impossible task as the sole means of their salvation. This would insure, like Sisyphus' plight, that they will fail, and liberation collapses into an unrealizable hope.

On the basis of the evidence already marshaled, it is safe to say that the inevitability and perpetuity of black suffering, and God's responsibility for it, at least raise the issue of divine racism. And the reader should keep in mind that this is my primary concern: to show that the black theologian must consider and demolish the charge of divine racism, because his own position makes it a threshold issue.

Washington can avoid the conclusion that God is a white racist only because he brings to his analysis the presupposition that black suffering is evidence of divine favor. But the one component that must be corroborated to support his interpretation—the exaltation-liberation event for blacks—is missing from his evidence. He affirms God's favor relative to blacks only by begging the question, since the perpetuity of suffering contradicts this relation. In summary, we cannot avoid the question of whether the conditions Washington advances as evidence of God's favor do not represent the identical state of affairs one would expect if God were a white racist.

"God, Do It Yourself."

Even if the features of inevitability and perpetuity were excused, there would remain yet another fatal flaw in Washington's theodicy: it appeals to a servant soteriology, or to be blunt, a slave soteriology. The image that comes to my mind in reading Washington is that of the faithful, involuntary slave who gives his all for the life and safety of his master, hoping all the while that his freedom will follow his faithful execution of his assigned task. I have visions of a slave rushing into a burning house to save the master's child, spurred on by the master's promise of freedom if the rescue is successful—and if he survives.

There is simply no way to avoid the conclusion that blacks are suffering for whites in Washington's system; that black suffering, as he affirms, is "intercession for the transgressors." For transgressors, simply substitute white oppressors. Indeed he acknowledges that blacks are God's only "promised hope for white rebelliousness which deserves death and destruction."[30] Without black suffering, whites are doomed to divine annihilation. If blacks, the innocent in Washington's scheme, must undergo suffering, in fact more suffering than the "bad guys," if blacks are the necessary means for white deliverance, if our stripes and death are their means of salvation, then the question must be put, Where is God's real loyalty; does He have real regard for blacks themselves or is He simply using them for a higher end—the highest good of whites?

This question is all the more significant precisely because Washington castigates white racism as a religious and moral abomination and an unpardonable affront to the very nature of God. One cannot but ask why God does not exercise overruling sovereignty to expunge white racism as He exercises it to make blacks the suffering servant. It is already clear that Washington does not emphasize God's respect for human freedom as the explanation of black suffering. Thus he must answer this question: Why does God respond to the *sin* of white

racists by making the suffering of *innocent* blacks the means
of white *salvation?* Washington's suffering-servant theodicy,
I submit, makes white non-suffering inexplicable.

At this point it must be said in Washington's behalf that
the duality of black suffering—the vicarious suffering of blacks
is the means by which blacks themselves are liberated—is designed to answer the charge of divine racism. This, however,
does not provide the necessary support. I contend that the
vicarious suffering of blacks is intended more for white salvation than for black liberation, for does not black liberation
hinge upon the success of liberating whites from bondage to
preconscious racism? In this respect, one should accent Washington's interpretation of black slavery in America; it is a
necessary component of the black mission for white salvation:

> Slavery with eventual emancipation has too long been
> misconstrued as the end rather than the beginning to
> which God has called the Negro people of America.
> Slavery was but the means for inextricably binding the
> Negro and the Caucasian. Without this binding the im-
> measurably more bruising work of releasing whites from
> their blasphemous bondage to whiteness and racial su-
> periority cannot be done.[31]

One cannot but be astounded at this admission, but, again,
this view of slavery is inescapable once Washington affirms his
rigid doctrine of God's sovereignty relative to human freedom. Is he not affirming that, were it not for white rebelliousness, black slavery would not have been necessary? Is not
God here ultimately responsible for slavery in the manner that
Rubenstein sees Hitler as God's agent, for it is an indispensable part of the salvation plan He inaugurates and sustains?

In this connection, it is also instructive to pinpoint the striking difference between the respective roles of Jews and of
blacks as suffering servant in Washington's scheme. Whereas
God's purpose demanded the release of the Jews from their

Egyptian oppressors, His mission for blacks excludes a similar Exodus:

> If the will of God for His people Israel demanded in their time of travail their departure from the land of Egypt through His mysterious purpose, the will of God for His Negro people demands no exodus. For God has called the Negro people to an infinitely more complex and responsible task—not only of being released from bondage but of releasing its captors from their shackles as well.[32]

One must not miss the point that the universal mission of the Jews omits the particular mission of converting their Egyptian oppressors to monotheism and releasing them from their "blasphemous bondage" to polytheism and heathenism. Nor was their exodus contingent upon the successful completion of their mission. Washington argues that blacks must continue their vicarious suffering in the land of the oppressor until whites become what God intends them to be. Could the contrast between the biblical model Washington claims to honor and the black plight be more pointed?

I think it is only reasonable and appropriate for blacks to question, if not distrust, the motives and purpose of a God who demands the type of suffering Washington sanctions, especially when a commensurate suffering is not extracted from whites, who deserve, in his own words, "death and destruction." The only response to Washington's God is the now familiar words, "Hell, no, I won't go!" or "God, do it Yourself."

On the basis of all that has been argued thus far I conclude that Washington's treatment of black suffering does not refute divine racism but reasserts it with a vengeance. Full weight must be given to the fact that the core of black suffering issues as much—I would say more—from God's choice of blacks as His suffering servant as from white racism. God's selection of vicarious suffering as the means of salvation forces the same conclusion. In addition, Washington provides another entrance for divine racism when he argues that God's reason for selecting blacks as His suffering servant "is no more fathomable than

his choice of Israel to be His suffering servant."[33] This appeal
to the mystery of God's ways is nothing more than a variant
of the "beyond human comprehension" strategy, which has already been criticized. If there is a mystery regarding the *reason* for the selection, is not the *purpose* for the selection also
engulfed in mystery? To the degree that God's reason and
purpose are unfathomable, to the same degree divine racism
is a viable interpretation. And if we add the perpetuity and
inevitability of black suffering, along with the instrumental
role of blacks for the white oppressor's salvation, Washington
has, perhaps unintentionally, given us a possible clue to the
cause of black suffering: "Negroes can only perceive themselves
to be afflicted by God."

Washington appears to combine two categories that should
be kept separate: divine election and divine benevolence. In
the context of divine racism, their combination is question-
begging. Having assumed God's intrinsic goodness as he does,
any election must have a benevolent purpose; it must enhance
the welfare of the elect. But election, like suffering, is multievidential. It can be for the woe as well as the welfare of the
chosen. We cannot determine which is the case by virtue of
the fact of the election itself; surely this is circular. In
the context of divine racism, God would elect blacks, but as the
object of His scorn and hostility, not of His loving grace.

I receive the strong impression now that Washington has
completely reversed his position about the radical duality of
the black mission. This is clear when one compares the theology of suffering that informs *The Politics of God* and a later
discussion of the black mission in a recent article, "How Black
Is Black Religion?" In this article he appears to reduce the
black mission to spearheading its own liberation; freedom of
the black man becomes the single overriding, if not the exclusive, salvific role for blacks:

> The particular responsibility of black churches is to con-
> tribute to the needs of black people and therefore to the
> society as a whole. In fact black churches have no other

responsibility than to contribute to the freedom of black people. . . .

It is my conviction that freedom is the heart and whole of the black church, the essence of the black church is freedom. The loyalty of the black church is to the Lord of history. The test of the quality of black existence is freedom. Without freedom black people will perish and with them their neighbors. Only by the increase of freedom among black people is there an opportunity for dynamic peace open in the future.[34]

I applaud this new direction in Washington's thought, but it is clear that it can be maintained only by a complete scrapping of the theology of suffering in *The Politics of God*. Since his later position effectively eliminates the suffering-servant motif and with it the theodicy of vicarious suffering, the problem of black suffering relative to the Lord of history becomes even more acute: How is Washington to account for the inequality of black suffering now? How can he explain black slavery in America? Black suffering, especially in the past, is even more inexplicable in the new framework that Washington advances.

The Least Attractive Theodicy

It is obvious that I find little merit in the suffering-servant theodicy. In fact, I regard it as the least attractive theodicy for a black theology of liberation. Its defects, which are dramatically illustrated by Washington's position, can now be summarized:

(1) Before the theodicy of vicarious suffering can be legitimately utilized, the theodicy of deserved punishment must first be convincingly refuted. This follows from the fact that his excess suffering cannot be deserved. The difficulty of this demonstration has already been described.

(2) Given the multievidentiality of suffering, the employ-

ment of the theodicy of vicarious suffering requires another difficult demonstration: One is pushed either to regard all suffering as vicarious or to provide the criterion for differentiating between redemptive and non-redemptive suffering. This distinction is critical, for the suffering associated with redemptive suffering must be embraced and endured. On the other hand we can attack and exterminate non-redemptive suffering. There can be no question that such a criteriology regulated Martin L. King's position, for instance. He regarded certain suffering, e.g. poverty, as non-redemptive and accordingly sought its elimination. But nowhere is the guide for separating redemptive from non-redemptive suffering made explicit.

(3) The theodicy of redemptive suffering collapses into a form of quietism. To make suffering redemptive is to give it a positive quality; it is to endow it with a high salvific quotient, with the obvious consequence that few moves will be taken to annihilate it. And when one considers the difficulty involved in differentiating between redemptive and non-redemptive suffering, this shortcoming becomes more weighty.

(4) The dangers of the theodicy of vicarious suffering for a black theology of liberation become even clearer when we note the tendency of certain theologians to advance the model of the suffering servant as the central Christian and Christological model. Once the black Christian concludes that God Himself has died and suffered for the other, how can he refuse to follow in His footsteps? How can he avoid James Cone's conclusion:

> By emphasizing the complete self-giving of God in Christ . . . the oppressors can then request the oppressed to do the same for the oppressors. If God gives himself without obligation, then in order to be Christian, men must give themselves to the neighbor in like manner. Since God has loved us in spite of our revolt against him, to be like God we too must love those who . . . enslave us. . . . This view of love places no obligation on the white oppressors. . . . In fact, they are permitted to do whatever they will

against black people assured that God loves them as well as the people they oppress.[35]

Rather than embracing the suffering-servant theodicy, the black theologian must firmly insist that the prerequisites for redemptive suffering are not part of the black situation.

VII

JAMES CONE: GOD, CHAMPION OF THE OPPRESSED

Cone's theodicy provides an illuminating comparison and contrast to Washington's. On the one hand he unconditionally rejects Washington's primary model of vicarious suffering and substitutes what, for him, is a more central biblical pattern. Here the two stand at opposite poles of the theological spectrum. On the other hand, the logical structure of Cone's theodicy is in fact identical to Washington's, and the same fatal flaws that infected Washington's reasoning are also present in Cone's. Like Washington, Cone fails to corroborate the event of black liberation that the validity and soundness of his position require. Cone's refutation of the theodicy of deserved punishment is ineffectual, and again like Washington, the consistency of his viewpoint is seriously endangered. At the heart of Cone's theodicy, too, is a question-begging component—the concept of blacks as the oppressed.

The validity of Cone's theodicy can be more accurately appraised and its more subtle shortcomings pinpointed if we discuss first the specific theodicies he rejects and the grounds for the rejection.[1] This is of critical importance, for this taking of a position through the process of eliminating indefensible theodicies establishes the logical and theological boundaries within which he must operate—if he is to be consistent. It is at this point that what is peculiar to his own thinking might be expected to emerge and assume command of his system.

Every criticism or refutation presupposes a critical apparatus or norm on the basis of which the object under analysis is said to be acceptable or not. For Cone, any theodicy that "reconciles the oppressed to unjust treatment committed against them"[2] must be rejected. Stated positively, whatever advances the goal of black liberation, which is to say, the liberation of the oppressed, is suitable for a black theodicy. Thus the pro-liberation quotient of the theodicy in question appears to be his functional norm. If this is not the case, it is difficult to account for the summary manner in which he discards well-known theodicies with an impeccable biblical ancestry, such as the theodicy of vicarious suffering and the theodicy of deserved punishment.

The Refutation of the Theodicy of Vicarious Suffering

God, Cone maintains, has not chosen blacks "for redemptive suffering but for freedom." They are not "elected to be Yahweh's suffering people." Rather, they are elected because they are oppressed[3] "against [their] will and God has decided to make [their] liberation his own."[4]

Two different claims can be extracted from his statements here, and Cone appears to endorse both. Blacks are not chosen to suffer for the other, that is, the white oppressor. The other-directed impulse of the suffering servant is replaced with a self-sacrificing love for oneself and the black nation. There is no hint of the duality of black suffering in Cone's analysis. In fact, suffering for the other, in his understanding, can only be regarded as a feature of God's disfavor.

The statements also yield the interpretation that blacks are not chosen to suffer. Rather, the exact opposite must be affirmed: their election signifies their eventual liberation from the suffering that defines oppression. Indeed it would appear that the continued suffering of blacks, from Cone's perspective, is tantamount to the claim that God is a white racist. "God cannot be the God of black people and also will their suffering,"[5] be it redemptive or not. For this reason, then, substantiating the exaltation-liberation event for blacks, i.e. that which terminates black oppression, is mandatory for Cone.

It appears, however, that the suffering implicit in vicarious suffering is not what Cone finds abhorrent, for he explicitly allows that God's election of blacks for eventual liberation entails unavoidable suffering. He admits that the suffering involved in "the struggle for liberation" is inescapable. Moreover, he acknowledges that this type of suffering is central to the biblical perspective and the Church's account of the earthly ministry of Jesus:

> The relationship between freedom and suffering is . . . evident in the biblical tradition. The election of Israel is a call to share in Yahweh's liberation. . . . To be Yahweh's people, Israel must be willing to fight against everything that is against this liberation. . . . This involves suffering, because liberation means a confrontation between evil and the will of him who directs history. The existence of Jesus also discloses that freedom is bound up with suffering. It is not possible to be for him and not realize that one has chosen an existence in suffering.[6]

Thus it appears that the real object of Cone's theological scorn is suffering for the other when the other is the *oppressor*. Indeed to affirm vicarious suffering for the oppressor would contradict his doctrine of God. Moreover, it would mean that the work of God and the activity of the Christian would be at cross purposes. This can be affirmed because God intends the destruction of the oppressor, not his salvation. And God can do no other, in Cone's scheme, because His essence is to be against oppression. Cone expresses God's annihilating wrath against oppression and the oppressor at several key points:

> Black theology will accept only a love of God which participates in the destruction of the white enemy.[7]

What we need is the divine love as expressed in Black
Power, which is the power of black people to destroy their
oppressors here and now by any means at their disposal.
Unless God is participating in this holy activity, we must
reject his love.[8]

It would be necessary to reject God's love, because to permit
oppression to remain would signify that God's nature is not
to be for the oppressed; rather, it would reveal that God is
a God of racism. Thus Cone's rejection of vicarious suffering,
based on God's nature and purpose, requires that he substantiate the definitive liberation event for blacks.[9]

To make the same point in another way: Cone must repudi-
ate a theodicy of vicarious suffering, because God's love is restricted to the oppressed. It is worth noting that the black
theologians who endorse vicarious suffering also affirm God's
universal love, His concern for the salvation and well-being of
both the oppressor and the oppressed. The explicit universalism
of Washington has already been documented. We will see that
J. Deotis Roberts' emphasis upon liberation and reconciliation
as the twin purposes of God moves in the same direction. A
similar accent illustrates the thought of Major Jones, and this
will receive proper attention in due course.

But, for Cone and Albert Cleage, God is not for all; they
replace His universal love with a radical particularity of concern:

In the New Testament, Jesus is not for all, but for the
oppressed, the poor and unwanted of society, and against
oppressors. . . . Either God is for black people in their
fight for liberation and against the white oppressors, or
he is not. He cannot be both for us and for the white oppressors at the same time.[10]

In sum, to assert God's universal love for both the oppressed
and the oppressor is to make God a monstrously immoral Dr.
Jekyll and Mr. Hyde.

Cone's argument for the essential unity of God's love and

God's wrath, God's love and God's righteousness goes hand in hand with his rejection of the theodicy of vicarious suffering. It is necessary to elevate God's wrath to co-ordinate rank with his love, because of the actual and potential theological abuse that comes from an exclusive emphasis upon God's love, especially self-sacrificing love. Once God's wrath is divorced from His love, the oppressed must submit to the oppressor's dehumanizing activity without reprisal, with only verbal condemnation or, as it were, a slap on the wrist. "A God without wrath does not plan to do much liberating, for the two concepts belong together."[11]

However, there are several ways of interpreting the unity of God's love and His wrath, and it is not always clear which of them Cone intends. But it is unmistakable which of the two interpretations is mandatory for the inner consistency of his position. One can argue that God's love for X requires His opposition to non-X. This approach appeals to the principle that every affirmation involves a negation, expressed here as all those persons who frustrate God's plan for X. This view informs Cone's claim that God's love for the oppressed dictates His destruction of the white oppressor. The consequence of his theological stance is to push God's wrath in the direction of retributive punishment; His wrath aims at the ultimate destruction of the oppressor, and not his salvation.

The connection between divine love and divine righteousness can be interpreted in yet another way: In this context God's wrath is remedial and redemptive. This view corresponds roughly to the position already considered where suffering or punishment is a sign of God's favor; suffering indicates what He sanctions and what He opposes, and thus serves as a guide to the straight and narrow path of salvation.

This redemptive, in contrast to the retributive, interpretation does not appear to be Cone's view, for to advance it would push him much closer to Roberts. It would require that he, like Roberts, must advance both liberation and reconciliation as the core of the gospel, rather than emphasizing almost exclusively the theme of liberation as Cone does. Cone would also have to argue that the "destruction" of the white oppressor is in fact related to his eventual salvation.

Several crucial consequences follow from Cone's claims that God has elected blacks not for vicarious suffering but liberation and that God's wrath involves the destruction of the white oppressor. If he adopts the retributive interpretation—and this is my understanding—it becomes all the more imperative for him to substantiate the definitive event of black liberation. If he does not do this, he will be in this curious and embarrassing situation: Having rejected vicarious suffering, which allows for a surplus of suffering for the elect, he is forced to define the white oppressor as the object of God's scorn, though it is the oppressive situation of blacks that corresponds, perhaps more closely, to that status. Cone is now pushed to prove his point by shifting the surplus of suffering from blacks to whites. There must be a reversal of roles, with whites now the primary sufferer. A cursory reading of history and the actual black experience, past and future, seems to contradict this position.

By emphasizing God's wrath as destruction, Cone inadvertently affirms the theodicy of deserved punishment as the explanation for certain occurrences of suffering. Having made this allowance, it becomes a possible explanation for black suffering as well. Accordingly it becomes all the more crucial for him to show that black suffering is not deserved punishment. Indeed, having repudiated the theodicy of deserved punishment, the refutation of deserved punishment is even more imperative for Cone than for Washington. Strictly speaking, the real mystery of mysteries in Cone's system is the *origin* of black suffering. For if God is for blacks, if their suffering is neither vicarious nor merited punishment, whence their suffering in the first place?

The Refutation of the Theodicy of Deserved Punishment

In addition to the theodicy of vicarious suffering, Cone also dismisses the theodicy of deserved punishment—but on radically different grounds. It hardly needs saying that the validity of his treatment of black suffering requires an unmistakable demonstration that the suffering he connects with oppression is not punishment for prior sin. What he actually establishes are some dubious epistemological canons, and these are totally incommensurate to the logical demands of his theodicy.

His first epistemological claim is that whites cannot make any valid judgment about black sin; they therefore cannot legitimately judge whether black suffering is the result of prior sin. "The oppressors are in no position to speak about the sinfulness of the oppressed. Black theology rejects categorically white statements about the sins of black people, suggesting that we are partly responsible for our plight." And again in the same vein: "White people are not permitted to speak about what blacks have done to contribute to their condition."[13]

This conclusion about the perceptive judgment of whites is joined with a second epistemological claim about blacks, namely that sin is a "community concept" and accordingly "only black people can speak about sin in a black perspective."[14]

My purpose here is not to challenge the adequacy of the foregoing claims; rather, I wish to question the validity of Cone's refutation of the theodicy of deserved punishment. I contend that the aforementioned epistemological claims do not rebut the view that black suffering is the consequence of prior sin.

Let us grant for the sake of argument that whites cannot legitimately talk about black sin and consequently are without grounds for describing black suffering as merited punishment. All that Cone can establish by this claim is who is not competent to decide if black suffering is deserved punishment. Granted that an answer from the white side is neither legitimate nor possible, this simply means that the answer must be given by blacks. It does not mean, as Cone appears to conclude, that the question need not be answered at all.

As a matter of fact, once the issue of divine racism is raised, as Cone himself raises it, it is necessary to show that the suffering at issue is not deserved or a sign of divine disfavor. To be sure, the special epistemological status he assigns to blacks is undermined as long as the interpretation of deserved punishment is not decisively rebutted. For until Cone confirms that punishment for sin is not the case, he cannot establish the major plank of his theodicy: blacks are the oppressed, a group with a special and favored relation to God.

Note the core of Cone's argument here. It is by virtue of their status as the oppressed that blacks occupy the unique epistemological position that makes them sole judge of the character of their sin and its relation to their suffering. However, without a persuasive refutation of the theodicy of deserved punishment, the classification of blacks as oppressed clearly begs the question, and Cone's theodicy is invalid until this flaw is eliminated.

Other Defective Theodicies

Cone's eventual statement of theodicy is shaped also by his refutation of other classical theodicies. He repudiates any treatment of black suffering that appeals to God's inscrutable will or transports the rationale for black oppression to a sphere beyond human comprehension. He also rejects any appeal to an eschatological compensation for earthly suffering, though there may be an inconsistency on this point.[15] Two concerns motivate Cone here: One is to rebut divine racism. The other is to avoid those theodicies which are conceptual props for oppression, in particular quietism.

It is now necessary to indicate the general theological viewpoint that, for Cone, provides support for the ideology of oppression. The specific position he attacks is Emil Brunner's concept of divine providence. Brunner's position, according to Cone, reduces to the following propositions:

All that is, and all that happens, takes place within the knowledge and the will of God. . . . All that happens is connected with the divine purpose; all is ordered in accordance with, and in subordination to, the divine plan and the final divine purpose.[16]

Over against this position Cone wants to affirm the concept of God that must inform an authentic black theodicy: "Black theology cannot accept any view of God that even *indirectly* places divine approval on human suffering."[17]

To clarify the issues introduced by Brunner's statement and Cone's counterstatement it is helpful to compare and contrast the respective theodicies of Cone and Rabbi Richard Rubenstein. Rubenstein would agree with Cone that Brunner's concept of divine providence leads to the "theological obscenity" of making Hitler God's redemptive agent and the slaughter of six million Jews His will. He also, like Cone, wants to avoid the conclusion that God is demonic, an anti-Semite, or responsible for the crimes of human history. Rubenstein concludes that the only way to steer clear of this conclusion is to abandon the theological hypothesis of God's activity within and God's sovereignty over human history or both. It is for this reason that Rubenstein introduces a concept of God with only minimal connection to human history.

Cone, however, wants to retain the sovereignty of God over human history and His activity within it and yet avoid the damaging consequences of this affirmation in Brunner's thought. Cone seeks to accomplish this theological sleight of hand by restricting God's sovereignty or activity to selected events of human history, those areas in which the oppressed are liberated.

Cone's instincts are surely understandable from a pragmatic viewpoint and even from a psychological perspective. But theologically, and especially logically, his position is not tenable. This becomes clear if we isolate the two opposing demands he tries unsuccessfully to honor: One demand of a black theology of liberation is to insure that blacks will assign only a negative quality to their oppressive suffering and thus provide the necessary motivation for its elimination. A second demand is to hold fast to God's sovereignty at all costs, for to deny His omnipotence is to annihilate black hope and to plunge blacks into the quicksand of defeatism. In point of fact, the same conclusion would follow from the conviction that God is a white racist, and it is for this reason that the refutation of divine racism becomes a primary enterprise for the black theologian.

Cone's argument for a belief "in the future reality of life after death" explains his reason for clinging to God's sovereignty as an indispensable cornerstone for black theology. "Blacks can fight against overwhelming odds," because they believe that the future is in fact the future of God, the liberator of the oppressed. Accordingly victory over oppression, evil, and death is assured. But, once the belief in immortality is challenged, then

> All is despair. The guns . . . and every conceivable weapon of destruction are in the hands of the enemy. By these standards all seems lost. But there is another way of evaluating history. . . . If we really believe that death is not the last word, then we can fight, risking death for the freedom of man, knowing that man's ultimate destiny is in the hands of him who has called us into being.[18]

This view of sovereignty creates special problems for Cone. He agrees that God's controlling or overruling sovereignty must be affirmed relative to human history or the eschaton. But this conclusion automatically raises the question of why God's overruling and controlling sovereignty does not operate where the crimes of human history are involved. Cone is now required to answer how white racism thrives within the larger freedom and sovereignty of God. If white racism runs rampant while God is allegedly "in control," where then is the basis for black hope?

Cone's actual position is obscure regarding these issues. Strictly speaking, he equivocates between two different and opposed concepts of divine transcendence, utilizing one or the other where it most easily fits the particular argument at hand. The passage just cited suggests God's overruling and controlling sovereignty, and accordingly His plan for the liberation of the oppressed will never be frustrated.[19] Other passages affirming the same point may be readily cited. But this line of argument pushes him directly into Brunner's theological camp, which he rejects with such vehemence.

Dr. Cone also employs a concept of divine transcendence that appears to be identical to essential features of humanocentric theism. At the primal level of reality, at the ontological level, God is sovereign. But, at the level of human history, He exercises his omnipotence by making man a codetermining partner, thus giving man, as it were, functional control over human history. God retains His sovereignty at both the ontological and the historical levels, but He refuses to exert his power in an overruling fashion in human history out of respect for man's freedom. Thus God's sovereignty is not functionally ultimate relative to human history, but this, as we will see, negates the view that His plan of liberation for the oppressed will necessarily come to fruition.

Let us take the argument one step further. Recognize that the issue of divine transcendence raises the question of God's knowledge and will relative to human suffering in general and black suffering in particular. With this understanding, several features of Cone's argument fall into place. We understand his reason for affirming that God does not "even indirectly" approve of human suffering, and we understand how various parts of his position feed into that assertion. If he argues that God approves of some instances of human suffering but not all, he is forced to provide the criterion to differentiate between what is approved and what is unapproved suffering. Merely to state the problem identifies its difficulty.

His more universal claim, namely that God does not approve of human suffering even indirectly, has several advantages: It does not necessitate the criteriology just cited. It also serves admirably another demand of a theology of liberation: to give a negative quality to the suffering implicit in oppression. But it runs afoul of Cone's affirmation regarding God's controlling sovereignty. If God abhors human suffering, then how are we to account for its actual presence? The fact of suffering calls into question the sovereignty of God, or else it suggests that

He is not exercising His transcendence for the good of black liberation.

Cone's desire to restrict God's activity and God's sovereignty in history to the liberation of the oppressed, while tracing the oppression itself to other causes, such as white racism, is understandable. In this way he establishes that God does not approve of black suffering; hence, an implicit refutation of divine racism. But is his theological strategy successful here? I think not. If his approach is not to be offensively arbitrary, if it is to avoid a self-serving strategy that permits him to choose the events that fit his theory and simply dismiss the contrary evidence, he is bound to provide specific arguments for his case.

His strategy is not possible without the unwarranted presupposition of God's intrinsic goodness relative to blacks or at least a citation of the mighty acts of God relative to black liberation. Cone's strategy also presupposes that where the biblical God of history is active in human affairs, He is pursuing a benevolent purpose for the oppressed. But once Cone has defined the issue as he did initially—a God of racism or a God of liberation—he cannot begin his analysis with these two presuppositions. Rather, they must be conclusions demonstrated. In sum, Cone must first refute one of the two interpretive options he outlines, before he can reasonably affirm the other. He is required to disprove the charge of divine racism, to identify what he regards as the definitive event(s) of black liberation, and also to refute the theodicy of deserved punishment.

Cone faces similar methodological demands because of his rejection of specific theodicies and the grounds for those rejections. Having discarded the theodicy of deserved punishment and denied that God is a white racist, Cone effectively precludes any interpretation of black suffering as a sign of divine disfavor. Hence he is forced to operate in the framework of suffering as a sign of divine favor. But this, too, pushes the necessity of an event of black liberation to the forefront.

In sum, Cone's rejection of the defective theodicies makes it difficult for him to account for the maldistribution and the very origin of suffering, which is the starting point of his theological construction. The position he assumes relative to these theodicies also obliges him to identify the definitive event of liberation for blacks. The discussion of these issues as they relate to divine racism must now be discussed.

Are Blacks Oppressed?

The core of Washington's theodicy was summarized in the following syllogism:

> If Blacks are the suffering servant / chosen people, then God is not a white racist.
> Blacks are in fact the suffering servant / chosen people.
> _____
> Therefore God is not a white racist.

Cone's theodicy can also be reduced to syllogistic form:

> If blacks are the oppressed, then God is not a white racist.
> Blacks are obviously the oppressed.
> _____
> Therefore God is not a white racist.

A comparison of these syllogisms indicates that Cone's theodicy has the same logical structure. Cone puts forward a class that _by virtue of his stipulative definition_ involves a favored and specialized relation to God. Whereas Washington posited the class of suffering servant, Cone advances the class of the oppressed. Thus the soundness of Cone's argument stands or falls on the demonstration of the second premise: blacks are oppressed. In this connection the reader must recognize that Cone adds a defining element to the concept of the oppressed that is question-begging in light of the issue of divine racism that he raises. Essential to his meaning of "oppressed" is the claim that they are the object of God's special concern and love. This stipulative meaning of "oppressed" thus constitutes an implicit "refutation" of the charge of divine racism. Consequently the real effect of Cone's arbitrary definition of "oppressed" is to eliminate, but only by definition, all the subclasses of divine disfavor, such as divine racism and deserved punishment. But this point cannot be emphasized too strongly; the refutation is the consequence of the classification and stipulative definition, and only that. In this context, then, the real issue for Cone reduces to this crucial question: Has he substantiated that blacks are in fact the oppressed? It is necessary to translate the last statement into the language of Cone's definition and thus identify the specific proposition he must validate. Has he substantiated that blacks are in fact *the object of God's favor?* Because of the common tendency to classify blacks as oppressed, and because common usage does not include Cone's stipulative property, namely that God is favorably inclined toward the oppressed, it is necessary to phrase the question as just stated to avoid begging the question. Because it is commonly held that blacks are oppressed, Cone's affirmation of the same proposition seems self-evidently certain, and the syllogistic statement of his theodicy appears logically impeccable. His argument accordingly presents itself with a logical certitude that it does not actually possess. For this reason, too, Cone's special and personalized definition of "oppressed" must be pinpointed.

Looked at from another perspective, Cone's theodicy and its implicit refutation of divine racism rest finally upon a doctrine of God's nature: "The liberation of the oppressed is a part of the innermost activity of God himself. This means that liberation is not an afterthought, but the essence of divine activity."[20] This is Cone's way of stating the classical theistic principle that goodness is intrinsic to God. It must also be indicated that the divine activity of liberation incorporates, as well, the work of Jesus Christ, especially the Resurrection.

It goes without saying that if liberation of the oppressed is in fact the essence of God's nature and action, divine racism is clearly excluded. It is not possible for a divine racist and a liberator of oppressed blacks to coexist in the same divine person. To appraise the validity of Cone's theodicy, then, demands that we examine his exposition for this specific description of God. He seeks to validate this description of God's

nature through three primary demonstrations, but they turn out
to be different ways of saying the same thing. That the liberation of the oppressed is the core of the biblical message and
of Israelite history is his first claim: "It is indeed the biblical
witness that says that God is a God of liberation, who calls
to himself the oppressed and abused . . . and assures them
that his righteousness will vindicate their suffering."[21]

The second demonstration appeals to Jesus' personhood and
work:

> In the New Testament, the Old Testament theme of libera-
> tion is reaffirmed by Jesus himself. The conflict with Satan
> and the powers, the condemnation of the rich, the insist-
> ence that the Kingdom is for the poor, and the locating
> of his ministry among the poor—these and other features
> of the career of Jesus show that his work was directed to
> the oppressed for the purpose of their liberation.[22]

Because of the biblical emphasis upon liberation, revelation
must also center around the liberation of the oppressed. This
is the third demonstration in his approach. It is necessary here,
for the sake of a subsequent criticism, to call attention to
Cone's emphasis upon revelation as grounded in concrete, i.e.
actual, events in which the community of the faithful detect the
liberating hand of God:

> In the Bible revelation is inseparable from history and
> faith. History is the arena in which God's revelation takes
> place. . . . The God of the Bible makes his will and
> purpose known through his participation in human his-
> tory. . . . Christianity . . . is a religion which affirms
> that we know who God is by what he does in the histori-
> cal events of man.[23] In fact, there is no revelation of God
> without history. The two are inseparable.[24]

A second passage must be cited in detail as background for
the claim that Cone's own doctrine of revelation, as well as
other essentials of his system, force him to identify the definitive event(s) of black liberation:

God chose to make himself known to an oppressed people, and the nature of his revelatory activity was synony-
mous with their emancipation. The Exodus of Israel from
Egypt meant that God's revelation was an act of liberation. In this revelatory event, Israel not only came to
know God as the liberator of the oppressed, but she also
realized that her being as a people was inseparable from
divine activity. Thus Yahweh was known primarily for
what he did for Israel when other political powers threatened her existence as a community. . . . God's revelation
means political emancipation, which involves the destruction of the enemy. . . . The entire history of Israel
is a history of what God has done, is doing and will do in
moments of oppression.[25]

The foregoing account of revelation forces the conclusion,
as Cone acknowledges, "There is no revelation of God without
a condition of oppression which develops into a situation of
liberation."[26] Only one meaning can be extracted from this
statement in particular and Cone's doctrine of revelation in
general: Revelation involves two necessary conditions. There
is (1) the event of suffering or oppression, which is replaced
by its opposite (2) liberation or exaltation. It should be noted
that these conditions are the same two elements already identified as central to the concept of suffering servant. Can we avoid
the conclusion here that Cone's own doctrine of revelation
affirms that in the absence of the liberation event there is no
revelation? And this is to say that there is no accurate knowledge of God's nature. Can we avoid the conclusion that knowledge of God's nature as liberator—and it must be remembered
that for Cone this is His essence—presupposes concrete instances of liberation? In like manner, can we affirm that black
liberation is part of God's innermost nature except on the basis
of the actual liberation of blacks?

Cone's concern to establish the nature of God as the primary
category for theodicy and his conclusion that revelation of
God's nature is mediated only through events of liberation

oblige him to adopt a particular theological method—if circularity is to be avoided. I would identify the following methodological requirements:

(1) The description of God's nature as favoring the oppressed cannot legitimately be part of the presuppositional baggage the theologian brings to his analysis. Rather, God's nature as favoring the oppressed must be validated. It also means that the theologian cannot use this description at the outset to dismiss the alleged counterevidence; rather, this description can stand only after the counterevidence has been refuted or shown not to be decisive.

(2) It also means that this view of God must be confirmed by the mighty acts of God, by an inspection of human history and the citation of those events in which God's liberating activity is claimed to be present, as, for example, in the Exodus. This is another way of saying that the theologian must identify actual events of liberation, concrete instances where the oppression in fact ceases, where, to use a metaphor of Cone's, "the last become first."

(3) The event of liberation must involve the liberation of the particular group in question; that is, an event of *Jewish* liberation cannot corroborate the claim that *black* liberation is part of God's innermost nature. The meaning of these last two methodological consequences will be clarified after the analysis below has exposed the question-begging features of Cone's concept of "oppressed."

(4) The final consequence to be identified has already been discussed in terms of the principle that God is the sum of His acts. The concern now is to show that Cone's controlling theological categories presuppose the same principle. Consider for instance his concept of revelation when he says: "There is no revelation without a condition of oppression which develops into a situation of liberation." Does not this claim entail that whatever character we assign to God must be substantiated by reference to His past and/or present acts? This especially appears to be the case because Cone has rejected any appeal to an eschatological compensation for suffering passed through

here and now. Consequently it appears that the only option for Cone is to speak of God as for the oppressed only on the basis of events of liberation in the past, the present, or in the process of actualization.

Consider some of the decisive statements from Cone himself that support this interpretation:

Black theology rejects the tendency of classical Christianity to appeal to divine providence. To suggest that black suffering is consistent with the knowledge and will of God and that in the end everything will happen for the good of those who love God is unacceptable to black people. The eschatological promise of heaven is insufficient to account for the earthly pain of black suffering. . . .[27] Providence is not a statement about the future. It is . . . a statement about present reality—the reality of the liberation of the oppressed.[28]

Cone's doctrine of God's immanence leads to the same conclusion: "The immanence of God . . . forces man to look for God . . . and make decisions about the ultimate in terms of present historical reality. Man cannot postpone his decision about God or condition it in terms of a future reality. The finality of God is his involvement in man's now experiences."[29]

Cone's claims that God does not indirectly approve of human suffering and that God is totally identified with black liberation also force him to identify the past or contemporary events of black liberation. How can blacks know that God disapproves of black suffering except by His elimination of it, except by His bringing it to an immediate halt?

Yet other statements by Cone demand a similar demonstration: "If God is truly the God of and for the oppressed for the purpose of their liberation, then . . . our movement in the world cannot be a meaningless thrust towards an unrealizable future, but a certainty grounded in the past and present reality of God."[30]

The same methodology must question Cone's use of the category "the oppressed" to describe blacks in America. When the meaning of oppressed in Cone's usage is laid bare, it is clear that Cone has not substantiated his claim that blacks are the oppressed. In this connection the reader must recall that Cone's own scaffolding requires the demonstration that blacks are the object of God's favor and that their liberation is central to His will.

Before the category of the oppressed can be used legitimately and accurately to describe blacks, it is necessary to demonstrate that the suffering they experience is not deserved punishment. Blacks can be indexed as oppressed only after it has been substantiated that their suffering is not merited. It is precisely at this point that the weakness of his refutation of the theodicy of deserved punishment returns to haunt Cone's system and render dubious his classification of blacks as oppressed.

If the conclusion is correct that the cessation of suffering, i.e. the liberation event, must occur to establish that suffering is undeserved, then Cone must identify what he regards as the definitive event of black liberation. Otherwise, there is no way to decide if black suffering is deserved punishment or unmerited suffering.

It must also be noted here that the positions Cone assumed to dismiss other theodicies severely hamper his theological maneuverability. His rejection of eschatological compensation, for instance, forces him to identify a contemporary or past event of black liberation. That the situation of blacks still requires radical correction indicates his classification is premature if not gratuitous.

Other problems confront Cone in his effort to identify the precise liberation event his position requires. To say that blacks are the oppressed is to say that God is or has been active in behalf of their liberation. This also means that Cone must show that the liberation of blacks is part of God's innermost nature. This cannot be accomplished by appealing to God's liberating activity for mankind in general or for non-blacks, such as the Exodus of the Jews. The Exodus may refute the charge of divine anti-Semitism, but it is irrelevant to the accusation of divine racism. What is demanded, then, is for Cone to specify concrete and definitive events of black liberation.

Other claims of Cone demand the same conclusion: He argues that we cannot know God "independently of his liberating work"[31] and, further, that knowledge of God as He is in Himself is not possible: "We can only know God in his relation to man, or more particularly in his liberating activity on behalf of oppressed man."[32] These twin claims allow us to speak of God as liberator only in terms of the concrete groups of the oppressed that he in fact liberates. Any other claim would be to talk of God "independently of his liberating acts." It would be similar to the argument that because Huey Long aided oppressed whites, he can be said to be the champion of oppressed blacks as well.

Albert Cleage clarifies the criticism here. He correctly recognizes the theological issue at stake: it is the scandal of particularity which is introduced by the character of black suffering and the accusation of divine racism. And the scandal of the particularity of black suffering can be answered only by an appeal to the particularity of God's liberating activity— an Exodus-type event for blacks. With this understanding, Cleage establishes God's liberating activity for blacks at the outset by arguing for the blackness of God, Jesus, and the Jews. The physical blackness of God and Jesus insures their identification with and participation in the struggle for black liberation. The blackness of the Jews guarantees that the Exodus is an authentic event of *black* liberation, the liberation of the particular group at issue.

Cone himself also recognizes that the Exodus is the liberation of a particular oppressed group and that a more universal event of liberation is required to accommodate the oppressed non-Jews. Is this not the import of the following passage, in which the Resurrection of Jesus is introduced as the universal event of liberation?

If the history of Israel and the New Testament description of the historical Jesus reveal that God is a God who is identified with Israel because she is an oppressed community, the resurrection of Christ means that all oppressed people become his people. Herein lies the universal note implied in the gospel message of Jesus. The resurrection event means that God's liberating work is not only for the house of Israel but for all who are enslaved by principalities and powers.[33]

But this confession is fatal to Cone's approach, for he is actually acknowledging that the biblical Exodus lacks any decisive import for the claim that the liberation of *blacks* is part of God's innermost nature. Unless he is willing, like Cleage, to make the Exodus an event of black liberation on the grounds that Jews are black, the Exodus is not available as evidence for his position. Indeed it would appear that the whole history of the Israelite nation as the object of God's liberating work is not relevant for his argument that God is involved in *black* liberation.

Thus he is left with the Resurrection as the crucial event for establishing that black liberation is part of God's nature. But even here one can question Cone's success in making the Resurrection a *universal* event of liberation and, by implication, an event of black liberation. Strictly speaking, is not the movement here, from the universal to the particular, to misunderstand the real issue of the charge of divine racism? He affirms the universal import of the Resurrection, but at no point does he indicate which of its features warrants its designation as an event of black liberation or of universal liberation. It would appear that Cone can speak of the Resurrection as a universal event only to the extent that particular groups are in fact liberated and only to the degree that liberation actually becomes or is in fact universal. Moreover, if we honor the suggestion that we can know God only in relation to man and in terms of His liberating acts, then we can speak of God as for *all* oppressed people only on the basis of the liberation of *all* oppressed people.

In point of fact, does not the continued suffering of blacks *after* the Resurrection raise the essential question all over again: Is God for blacks? We must not forget that black misery, slavery, and oppression—the very facts that make black liberation necessary—are all *post*-Resurrection events. Must not the fact of black oppression after the Resurrection raise the most serious questions about Cone's designation of the Resurrection as the event of universal liberation? It is closer to the truth, it seems, to say that Cone is affirming liberation in an unliberated world!

Still another claim of Cone makes problematical his classification of blacks as the oppressed. "Black theology," he argues, "cannot accept a view of God which does not represent him as being for blacks and thus against whites. . . . We must know where God is and what he is doing in the revolution. There is no use for a God who loves whites the same as blacks."[34] In the light of this assertion and the affirmation that God is only for the oppressed, can Cone show that God is on the side of blacks except by marshaling evidence for God's opposition to whites? It is embarrassing when we have to note that whites have been on top for aeons, apparently somewhat longer than Cone's purview of history permits. Moreover, the manner in which Cone structures the argument here makes it impossible to point to a progressive improvement for blacks and identify this as the liberation event if the status of blacks relative to whites has not significantly improved.

One final observation about Cone's theodicy is in order: If for the sake of argument we should allow his theodicy a gratuitous validity, a troublesome question would still remain unanswered. Indeed the greater his success in establishing that black liberation is essential to God's nature, the more troublesome this question would become: Whence comes the suffering of the oppressed in the first place if God is for the oppressed? How is the origin of black oppression to be accounted for? How is black slavery now to be squared with the claim that God has been and is on the side of blacks? The crucial issue in Cone's system is not the more traditional issue of original sin, but the original oppression of blacks.

On the basis of the foregoing arguments, I conclude that Cone has not certified the single proposition he himself affirms must be established if God is not a murderer: viz., black liberation is central to God's essence. In the absence of this demonstration, the remainder of the system totters for want of a convincing structural validity.

VIII

ALBERT CLEAGE: GOD, A BLACK SOUL BROTHER

It is unfair to analyze and criticize Albert Cleage's theodicy without some initial attention to the genre of his writing and accommodating the criticism to it. The focus of attention in this chapter is *The Black Messiah,* which comprises a selection of sermons delivered over an extended period. These sermons display a decided pragmatic flavor: to convert the audience to the cause of black liberation, to provide a theological rationale for specific goals and strategies of black liberation, and so on. In sum, the sermons should not be interpreted as theological treatises on the concepts upon which they tend to be focused.

For these reasons, one is never sure if he has accurately isolated and described Cleage's definitive position regarding a particular concept or whether a given concept and Cleage's treatment of it are called forth by the pragmatic needs of the sermon. For instance, his adoption of the framework of deserved punishment to analyze black suffering can easily, and perhaps ought to be, interpreted as an exercise in pragmatic theology[1] with the purpose in mind of motivating blacks to sacrifice everything for the liberation of the black nation.

In this sense it is not of the same character as Panaloux's theodicy of deserved punishment, considered earlier. Even to interpret it as a position in theodicy may well do violence to Cleage's actual meaning and purpose.

The fact that *The Black Messiah* is a collection of sermons also makes one question the legitimacy of selecting passages from different sermons to develop or to criticize a particular theme. What appear to be blatant contradictions may well reflect only the peculiar pragmatic needs and the motivational emphases of different sermons and the particular demands of dissimilar occasions.

I make these points to express a deep concern not to misinterpret Cleage's position by using it to answer a question he has not asked. No doubt the only fair method in this context is to consider his materials as *possible* theodicies that are *suggested* by his writings. In this way a vital issue is avoided that cannot be answered without additional and more systematic information from Cleage himself: namely, have we accurately presented his definitive theodicy?[2]

The Refutation of Divine Racism: God Is Black

Cleage does not explicitly consider the issue of divine racism, and the reason is not hard to discover. Given his manner of relating God and blacks, it would contradict his entire enterprise to even hint at the question, Is God a white racist?

The core strategy of his theodicy is to color God, Jesus, and the Jews (Israelites) black. God is not a racist, not only because He is *for* us blacks but also *like* us. In point of fact, Cleage affirms that He is for us only because we can assert that He is like us. What he says relative to Jesus applies as well to his doctrine of God. "Why do you think that a white Jesus would save you from the oppression of white men? That doesn't make sense. If he's their Jesus, he's saving them."[3]

Cleage's argument here is akin to that of the Reverend Buchner Payne, considered earlier. Strictly speaking, Cleage is arguing that to demonstrate that God is the savior of a particular group, it must be confirmed that God and that people are the same color. Hence Cleage's concept of salvation also makes it impossible for the issue of divine racism to emerge.

A comparison of Cleage's and Cone's positions is instructive at this juncture. Cone's concept of a black God emphasizes God's assumption of the *condition* of the oppressed, of siding with them and making their freedom the specific object of His saving work.[4] He is also willing to speak of blackness as a symbol of oppression when applied to God or Jesus Christ. Ontologically speaking, he also insists upon a black component in God in so far as He is the ground and Creator of the black man's humanity. However, I do not interpret him to affirm an identity of pigmentation between God and blacks. Strictly speaking, only Cleage's variety of black theology is a full-blown pigmentation theology.[5]

For Cleage, however, God's commitment to oppressed blacks and his total identification with them can be guaranteed only by establishing that God and the oppressed are physically or physiologically the same color. Anything less will severely restrict total identification and commitment; race is thicker than water. Being black, in short, is a necessary condition for God's unreserved allegiance to black liberation.

Though to be black is a necessary condition if God is in fact *for* black people, it is not, however, sufficient. God might be an "Oreo" God, black on the outside but white on the inside. Thus the only sufficient evidence of God's commitment to the black cause is His concrete activity in behalf of black liberation; there must be the event of black liberation and God its savage warrior. For Cleage, the revolutionary ministry of Jesus and the biblical Exodus of the Israelites are such events. It must be recalled that, having identified both Jesus and the Israelites as black,[6] these events become authentic occurrences of *black* liberation.

The identical color of blacks and God also establishes that blacks are the chosen people, and in this sense the category of the elect must be regarded as an implicit refutation of divine racism. Their status as God's elect guarantees their eventual liberation and insures that black genocide is not possible:

> Perhaps if we could just remember that we are God's chosen people, that we have a covenant with God, then we would know that God will not forsake us. . . . Because of this simple fact, the enemy is not going to destroy us.[7]

God Is Black: Problems and Prospects

The foregoing argument as a refutation of divine racism stands or falls upon the demonstration that God is black. Cleage grounds the claim of God's blackness upon a personalized interpretation of the category *imago dei,* man the image of God. This category, in Cleage's understanding, asserts that God comprises a "combination" of the actual characteristics of different groupings of mankind based on their respective numerical representation:

> . . . If God created man in his own image, then we must look at man to see what God looks like. There are black men, there are yellow men, there are red men and there are a few, a mighty few white men in the world. If God created man in his own image, then God must be some combination of this black, red, yellow and white. In no other way could God have created man in his own image.[8]

God, then, "must be a combination of yellow, black, red and with just a little touch of white; [accordingly] we must think of God as a black God."[9]

The characteristics of the people among whom His incarnation occurred also establish the blackness of God. That is, reading backward from the locus of His revelation, we can arrive at a precise picture of His nature. "If God were white . . . and if he decided to send his son to earth, he would have sent a white son down to some nice white people. He certainly would not have sent him down to a black people like Israel."[10]

If Cleage's argument is valid, the accusation of divine racism is without foundation and obviously collapses. Serious questions, however, can be raised about its validity. Allowing for every benefit of doubt, his argument establishes, at best, not that God is black but only that He is *non-white*. Throughout his writings Cleage employs non-white and black as if the two were equivalent expressions.[11] The implications of this approach for a Third World perspective are obvious. Non-white obviously comprises a spectrum of hues, which cannot be reduced to black. It is precisely at this point that the requirement of identity of skin color creates insurmountable problems. His position would be easier to defend if he had argued for the non-identity between God and the oppressor as regards color, rather than the identity of color between God and the oppressed.

But the real problem with Cleage's position is the *combination* interpretation of man as the image of God, for it is self-refuting. This becomes obvious once we raise the question, Should not the combination interpretation be applied to other characteristics as well? If it is legitimate relative to skin color, why not sex, height, weight, etc.?

Moreover, the combination approach ultimately undermines the claim that God is for blacks. The moment the combination rationale is applied, for instance to height, this would disrupt the previous groupings based primarily on skin pigmentation. Some blacks in the "in" group based on skin color would be excluded from the "in" population based on height.

Another serious problem is how to handle God's sexuality in a combination methodology. Does God become hermaphroditic or androgynous?

I do not wish to quibble, but the argument for God's blackness based on the locus of His incarnation is questionable. Surely it, like suffering and revelation, is multievidential. All the available black theologies overlook this point. They adopt the view that the locale of God's presence is a guarantee of

His favor toward the people in whose midst He appears. Yet an interpretation of disfavor is not to be summarily dismissed. Bernhard Forster, one of the leaders of the anti-Semitic movement in Germany, argued that Christ, an Aryan, appeared among the Jews, non-Aryans, because "on the dark background of the most depraved of nations, the bright figure of the Savior of the world would stand out the more impressively."[12] I would draw the following conclusion from all this: the crucial determinant of God's favor is not the *locus* of His incarnation or revelation, but what He *accomplishes* for the group in whose midst He appears. The liberation event is more critical, at least from the standpoint of theodicy, than the event of incarnation.

I would also conclude that the black theologian must avoid two extreme positions: his theodicy must be relevant to the elimination of the oppression of the group he represents; but he must avoid reintroducing the same oppression, reverse racism for example, or a different type of oppression, such as sexism. Cleage's response to white racism appears to fall prey to at least one of these dangers. His radical emphasis upon the importance of the particularity of God's incarnation will inevitably raise the issue of His incarnation in a specific human form, a male body. And here the issue of divine sexism becomes a live issue. What does Jesus' assumption of a male form imply relative to the coequal status, the cohumanity, and salvation of females?

A defect noted in Cone's system also emerges in Cleage's. How are we to explain black oppression at all if blacks are God's chosen people and if God Himself is black like us and therefore for us? This line of criticism, however, cannot be adequately developed until another aspect of Cleage's theodicy has been examined: black suffering as deserved punishment.

Black Suffering as Deserved Punishment

Cleage utilizes a specific theodicy that the other black theologians consciously avoid like the plague: the theodicy of deserved punishment. To see a black theologian advance this explanation of black suffering causes one to pause for several reasons. If the suffering is deserved, there is little or no basis for regarding whites as *oppressors*. All the blame in this interpretation falls squarely on blacks. They become totally responsible for their plight. Indeed this approach opens wide the door for regarding the white oppressor as God's agent of judgment.

Moreover, if the suffering is merited, is it proper to challenge it? No, we are obliged to endure it; any dodge presupposes that we are unwilling to accept the full weight of God's chastisement. In addition, to attempt to avoid the suffering would nullify the status of blacks as the suffering servant / chosen people in so far as we have noted that their innocence is a prerequisite. Consequently, on each point, the theodicy of deserved punishment appears to be counterrevolutionary, and it is for this reason, no doubt, that black theologians have openly and persistently forsaken it.

Cleage, however, interprets the concept in a way that seeks to skirt the dangers inherent in such a position. He attempts to elude the albatross of quietism that is commonly associated with a theodicy of deserved punishment. He seeks to accomplish this by making quietism itself the fatal sin and establishing an antithetical relation between sin and its correlative act of redemption. The degree of his success must now be determined.

The paradigm for his treatment of black suffering is the biblical account of the Israelites' wandering in the wilderness. "And your children shall be shepherds in the wilderness . . . and shall suffer for your faithlessness. . . ."[13] To make the Israelites shepherds in the wilderness instead of settling them in a fertile area is a form of punishment, and we are compelled to identify the antecedent sin. For Cleage, the Israelites were guilty of lacking sufficient courage, valor, and ferocity in their battle for the Promised Land. This failure involves an even more grievous sin: the failure to honor the duties of one made in the image of God. To be created in the image of God obliges man to defend his humanity at all costs. In this sense, the sin of the Israelites is a denial of a fundamental part of God's purpose for creation. Thus, given the severity of the sin, it is not strange to discover that the sins of the fathers are visited upon the children.

In like manner, blacks are being punished for their unpardonable quietism in the face of white oppression and for their failure to assert at all costs their God-given manhood by attacking ruthlessly every dehumanizing act visited upon them:

> The people who accept oppression, who permit themselves to be downtrodden, those people are faithless because God did not make men to be oppressed and to be downtrodden. And many times a man faces the choice between living as a slave and dying as a man. And when we choose to live as slaves, we are faithless and our children will be shepherds in the wilderness.[14]

Packed into this suggested theodicy are several presuppositions, which must be made explicit and examined. A specific view of God's righteousness, or the morality of the universe, is argued for. God demands an atoning act for *each* sin. He does not simply excuse human sin, but requires exact restitution. This is the case even when his chosen people are involved. Moreover, the act of restitution must be opposite in quality to the sin at issue, and the atonement must be the work of man himself. Finally, it is concluded that suffering continues until total satisfaction is rendered, and there is every likelihood that the children must compensate for the sins of their fathers:

> Some of you say, "If God is just, he ought to make it possible for us to go into the Promised Land right away.

We have suffered enough." God cannot wipe out our weakness and faithlessness to each other. We must make amends for more than one hundred years. For every moment of cowardice, when our grandfathers hid under their beds while black men died, there has to be a moment of courage before we dare think about entering a Promised Land. . . . For every moment of individualism, there must be a moment of togetherness. We cannot enter the Promised Land like this. There's too much blood on us. We still carry the mark of slavery.[15]

Having understood Cleage's reinterpreted theodicy of deserved punishment, one is still left with the sense that the strategy is a failure. The argument seems to crumble like Humpty Dumpty because of the enormous weight the category of deserved punishment is forced to support. It is understandable that Cleage would want to motivate his congregation to abandon the "turn the other cheek" ethic and to avoid the escapism characteristic of too much of the black past, and my criticism does not apply if this pragmatic concern exhausts his purpose. But if his analysis is interpreted as a theodicy of deserved punishment, it creates insurmountable hurdles, in particular the antithetical factor. Its shortcomings are so great that one must conclude that it is not serviceable as a black theodicy.

I, for one, find it difficult to isolate the precise sin that requires the degree and severity of suffering that blacks have encountered in America. Given all the failures of our forefathers to lynch the lyncher, one still feels a gross disproportion between black suffering and the alleged sin purported to be its punishment. The punishment appears to be a ten-fold retribution for the crime. Moreover, interpreting black suffering in this way fails to give proper weight to the efforts of our forefathers to oppose slavery and oppression with the limited options available to an enslaved people. When our Nat Turners and Denmark Veseys are placed on the scale, the disproportion is even more pointed. Nor can we fail to ask, Can this theodicy account for *all* black oppression on the basis of an antithetical relation between it and a prior sin? What is the prior sin for which the particulars of ghetto life, for example, are the antipodal suffering-punishment?

This strategy is also vulnerable when it tries to account for *white* non-suffering in the same categories. How are we to explain this in the context of Cleage's rigid principle of equal restitution for every sin? Where is the one-to-one punishment for white racism and white lynchings, which are the precondition for subsequent black sin and its consequent suffering? Are we to conclude that blacks have sinned more than whites in America? Could there be the maldistribution of suffering, which Cleage himself acknowledges, if his theodicy of deserved punishment were valid?

Indeed, white non-suffering appears to nullify his basic assumption that blacks are God's chosen people, in favor of the opposite claim, that whites are now His favorites. The fact that whites have gotten on top and stayed there is impossible to understand if blacks are the elect, especially in light of the following claims he makes in other sermons: "Anytime a people try to destroy God's chosen people, they are bound to find that desolation is their reward."[16] If we emphasize further his claim that God is willing "to break the very laws of the universe"[17] for his chosen people, the imbalance between black and white suffering strongly suggests that if blacks were ever the elect, whites have replaced them as God's darlings. In sum, the more he pushes the interpretation of black suffering as deserved punishment, the more inexplicable black misery is in relation to whites. Indeed, apparently only a wholehearted endorsement of an eschatological theodicy can rescue this theodicy from total collapse.

Another feature of Cleage's position should cause concern, for it seems to involve the perpetuity of black suffering. I have in mind his argument for strict parity between sin and punishment. Without a precise tabulation of the sins of our forefathers, there is no way to determine when adequate restitution has been made. His approach here leaves an opening for black suffering to continue until the eschaton, and this would all be in conformity with God's justice and love.

I would ask these questions: Can Cleage's position serve as a refutation of divine racism? Does Cleage's viewpoint suggest that God is a black God for black people, a black Uncle Tom, or a paleface deity? If God himself is black and for blacks, and if redemptive suffering and eschatological compensation are rejected, continued and disproportionate black suffering remains inexplicable in Cleage's own terms. Maybe his insistence upon a black God should force a reconsideration of theological dualism. Maybe there are two Gods, one white, one black, and the black God, like His children, is impotent to liberate His worshipers, because He is opposed by his white counterpart. Maybe the earthly black-white confrontation is simply a reflection of a transcendent state of affairs. Maybe . . .

IX

MAJOR JONES: MAN,
COSUFFERER WITH GOD

Several problems attend an examination of Major Jones's theodicy. First, his explicit discussion of theodicy is very sparse. If the analysis here were confined to it alone, a few pages would exhaust the materials. It is possible, however, to consider the key concepts of his thought, *black awareness* and a *black theology of hope,* as jointly constituting an implicit theodicy. This will be my approach.

The second problem in Jones's thought is an apparent contradiction between opposing concepts of God's sovereignty as it is manifested in human affairs. On the one hand he affirms a traditional view in black religion: "He's got the whole world in His hand." Over against this position he asserts a doctrine of God's sovereignty that requires the labor of man as a cosufferer. Before an analysis of his implicit theodicy can be considered, it is necessary to examine this basic inconsistency.

God: Omnipotent or Helpless?

Jones's explicit treatment of black suffering seems to parallel humanocentric theism, at least some of its essential premises.

He endorses Bonhoeffer's concept of man as cosufferer with God. God takes sides against suffering and evil but in such a manner that man's help is required to conquer evil:

> The God who lets us live in the world without the working hypothesis of God is the God before whom we stand continually. Before God and with God we live without God. God lets himself be pushed out of the world onto the cross. He is weak and powerless in the world, and this is precisely the way, the only way, in which he is with us and helps us. Matthew 8:17 makes it quite clear that Christ helps us not by virtue of his own omnipotence, but by virtue of his weakness and suffering.[1]

This resolution of human suffering avoids making God responsible for the crimes of human history. God is not responsible, because He is powerless to eliminate it by His own might —at least the manner in which He makes himself present among men involves a situation of impotence. As Jones himself argues, "God himself is helpless to relieve those who suffer at the hands of a ruthless enemy."[2] Thus a reduction of God's functional omnipotence permits an attendant abridgment of His responsibility for human oppression and suffering.

This resolution also effectively eliminates the view that God is acting in human history in a controlling way. He does not overrule or transmute the acts and decisions of men to obtain His own will and purpose. Rather, God enters history as a *man*, utilizing only that power that is consonant with His human status. God's causal responsibility, which would be the exercise of His overruling sovereignty, is thus diminished; the extent of his responsibility could not exceed that of any other man. At least these are the conclusions I would draw from Bonhoeffer's cryptic statements.[3]

The elimination of human oppression, then, is contingent upon man's opting to become a cosufferer with God. "Man cannot expect that God will come down from above and undo all wrongs for him."[4] Thus man must hold himself at least equally responsible for those moral evils that distort his institutions and corporate life.

When Jones seeks to remove God's overruling sovereignty from human history as the most appropriate vehicle for a black theodicy, I think his theological instincts are entirely correct. Yet he advances a different viewpoint, which contradicts this interpretation of human and divine coresponsibility for moral evil. The reason for the contradiction, no doubt, is his attempt to champion different purposes that may be incompatible.

In addition to establishing the principle of coresponsibility, he also seeks to provide theological motivation for blacks to undertake their liberation. Beyond this lies yet another goal: to isolate those theological concepts which can support a theology of hope, and it must be understood that a black theology of liberation, for Jones, must be grounded in a theology of hope.

The logical, theological, and psychological demands of a theology of hope lead inevitably to a strong affirmation of God's sovereignty. It requires a God who is in control of history, who's "got the whole world in His hand." If God's power is not sufficient to overcome white racism, blacks "are of all men most miserable." But to assign this degree of sovereignty to God raises, in turn, the question of His responsibility for black oppression.

The inconsistency becomes more pointed when we compare Jones's position in the following statements with his previous endorsement of Bonhoeffer's God, a helpless God who requires man's cosuffering to accomplish His task:

> Black people . . . have a right to hope only if in their eyes the world is full of all kinds of possibilities, namely all the possibilities ordained by the God of hope. Black people have a right to hope only if they see reality and mankind, white and black, in the hands of him whose voice calls into history from its end, saying, "Behold I make all things new. . . ."[5]

But, given God's helplessness and coresponsibility for human affairs, in what sense are reality and mankind in God's hands any more than in man's? Does not the concept of a "helpless" God require the assertion, "Behold we," i.e. God and man, "make all things new"?

Consider also the following passage, which outlines the concept of God demanded by an authentic black theology of hope:

> The goals of the black awareness movement will fall short of fulfillment if the movement is not rooted in a God of the future . . . who is strong enough to determine the outcome of the future both within and beyond history. . . . He must be a God who is active on man's behalf; he must be a God who is himself engaged in the cosmic battle with evil.[6]

Does not this passage presuppose the concept of God's overruling sovereignty, and is not this nullified by a view of the divine omnipotence operating only by virtue of "his weakness and suffering"?

Jones's analysis of divine wrath also appears to contradict his idea of a "helpless God":

> In the black community, God's righteousness is his power in relation to men who are not in the right, who do not do what is right, who violate the rights of others in self-righteous aggression. . . . This is not the way many black people see the white man's God. . . . Where God's love is not able to do its work freely, it employs other means such as protest, instruments of law, threats and punishment. At many points in history, God puts on the ugly mass of his wrath to pressure people to satisfy the needs of others even when they do not feel like it.[7]

One must ask whether the concept of God's wrath, as Jones describes it, has a legitimate place in a theology of God's helplessness. Is there logical harmony between the latter and the coercive factor of God's wrath to "pressure people to satisfy the needs of others even when they do not feel like it"? It is precisely at this point that the issue of divine racism surfaces, for it raises the question of God's wrathful activity regarding human oppression. If God does in fact act in a coercive fashion, if He has manifested His wrath in some areas, why has he not pressured whites to satisfy the basic needs of blacks? It appears that the helpless God in Jones's theodicy is the spit and image of the "white man's God," a divine racist who has not exercised His might decisively to improve black life.

The absence of God's coercive wrath in behalf of black liberation admits of several interpretations through which Jones can choose to escape the corner of divine racism. A theodicy of deserved punishment is consistent with both black misery and the absence of God's coercive wrath. The same is true for an eschatological theodicy, as well as the theodicy of redemptive suffering.

Seemingly Jones accepts Bonhoeffer's view that the Christian must suffer for the other. He approvingly cites the following passage from Bonhoeffer as a mature concept of God that the black Christian can use with merit: "The Christian is called to sympathy and action, not in the first place by his own suffering but by the suffering of his brethren, for whose sake Christ suffered."[8] Jones, however, does not inflate Bonhoeffer's suggestion into a full-blown theodicy of vicarious suffering. Rather, it appears that he actually contradicts Bonhoeffer elsewhere. Jones advances the priority of a healthy regard for self-fulfillment, urging the black man "to stand up and go after that which by God belongs to him."[9] I agree with Jones's emphasis upon the priority of self-interest and self-regard by the oppressed. I wonder, however, if it is possible to establish this principle if we begin with Bonhoeffer's emphasis upon the priority of regard for the other.

An Eschatology of Black Hope

It was suggested at the outset that the key concepts of Jones's thought involve an implicit theodicy. It is this theodicy which must now be looked at more closely. My major concern is to show that these key categories force the issue of divine racism and that the validity of his position requires the demonstration that God is not a white racist.

The controlling foci of Jones's theological position are the concepts of black awareness or black consciousness and the essentials of a black theology of hope. From one perspective, it is possible to make the theology of hope the controlling concept and thus regard black awareness as one of its essential elements. But we will misunderstand Jones if we fail to discern the relation between the theology of hope and his ultimate purpose, black liberation. In point of fact, it seems that the demands of black liberation actually dictate the content of his black theology of hope. In this sense, his theological interest is to identify the specific complex of concepts of God, man, ethics, etc. that a black theology of liberation must affirm.

The most appropriate place to begin is where Jones launches his own enterprise, with the concept of eschatology. A black theology of hope, he contends, must build upon a black eschatology, but this is not to be equated with the viewpoint of the current theologians of hope: Moltmann, Panneburg, and their school. A black eschatology aims "at a new correlation between the eschatological origins of Christian faith"[10] and the specific conditions, attitudes, and beliefs of blacks, who aim to be free. Specifically, a black eschatology must "hold within its content a promise to be redeemed within the earthly life span of those who possess such a hope."[11]

Another central pillar of a black eschatology must be an anthropology of hope. The theological requirement here is to provide an ontological analysis of man that illuminates the black man's situation as oppressive and at the same time arms him with a sense of worth, "the courage to be black," and the self-determination to take what is his rightful share of God's creation. It must also assert the possibility of the radically new and the transformation of this world's social structures.

Finally, a black eschatology must affirm that God possesses the appropriate attributes that are foundations for the possibilities of the future. In short, the nature and activity of God is the ontological scaffolding for an authentic black theology of hope. We have already noted one of the divine attributes that must inform black hope for the future: He must be active against evil and oppression. To this, two other features must be added: the *power of God* and the *visibility of His acts*.

An oppressed people, if they are to achieve their liberation, must see themselves as capable of changing the situation. Their self-image must include their self-affirmation as centers of power or freedom. To be fruitful, however, the power and freedom of man must be rooted in a larger power, the power of God:

> Black awareness commits its adherents to the power of God, whether affirmed or not. Through it alone can black people . . . join the human family by force of being-forward. Is this not freedom under God in its primary meaning? The exercise of such power will create the condition for meaningful relationships.[12]

Jones accents another dimension of the divine reality that has import for a subsequent criticism, namely that God's activity against evil and oppression must be confirmable in a visible way. To borrow the terms of my own thesis, there must be concrete events of black liberation. "For the black community, God must be at work in a visible sort of way. Especially, He must be seen in the progressive development towards a better social lot for a people oppressed."[13]

It is important to note the location of this statement in Jones's argument. It occurs immediately after his assertion that "God is the redeemer of the oppressed as well as of the oppressor; he joins the struggle on both sides, seeking to transform both the oppressed and the oppressor." This conjunction of statements is most significant, for it makes this point: A God who is for both oppressor and oppressed must still execute His power and love in a manner that progressively diminishes oppression. That is, to argue that He is for both still obliges one to demonstrate *visibly* that the situation of the oppressed is improving. And should it be added here, *relative to the op-*

pressor? Jones is to be commended for the forthright approach he takes in letting the actual history of blacks be the yardstick for measuring God's commitment to blacks. But the concept of God I find in his theology hardly squares with this measuring tool.

A Black Psychology of Hope

Having looked at some of the essentials of Jones's position, it is now possible to establish that he advances a number of arguments that are invalid without a refutation of the claim that God is a white racist. Consider, for instance, the core of his argument that the necessary framework for a contemporary black theology is a theology of hope. And Jones makes it clear that a black theology of hope presupposes that God supports and sponsors black liberation. It means that He abhors black suffering, that He is on the side of blacks, though not for blacks only. But what does this mean except that God is not a white racist, that He is not hostile to blacks?

If the previous argument is even close to the target, we are now permitted to conclude that black suffering surely raises the question of whose side God is on—if anyone's. Thus the minimal credentials for a black theology of hope appear to be the validation of God's power and benevolence relative to blacks.

Jones's actual approach, in contrast to his stated procedure, moves in a different direction. To put the point hypothetically, he expounds theologically the proposition that if a black theology of hope is to be more than mere wishful thinking, then God and man must possess characteristics X, Y, and Z. Thus his procedure makes explicit the specific propositions X, Y, and Z to be defended to formulate a theology of hope that leads to black liberation. But Jones never gets to the type of theologizing that his stated method and his conclusions dictate: the validation of the central propositions of his thought. He does not point to the concrete events or the special experiences that are the evidence for his claim. That God and man do in fact possess X, Y, and Z is never confirmed. Jones is like the strange lawyer who identifies the particulars of his case to be proved in his opening statement to the jury but suddenly rests his case at that point and retires from the floor.

To put it in another way, it is necessary to ask Jones if there are ample ontological and historical grounds for his black theology of hope. Where are the primal or normative experiences and occurrences that, in his view, confirm that God is for blacks? Is his theology of hope more akin to his description of the slave eschatology? Because slavery under the white oppressor completely destroyed the black people's hope in this world, the black man postulated "another reality beyond time and space"[14] to sustain himself in this worldly vale of tears. That is, the "reality" beyond space and time is not to be regarded as an actual structure of reality. Rather, it is a belief in the "unreal" that enables us to cope with the harsh tortures of the "real" world.

If this analysis of Jones's stated method is correct, then it seems that he is arguing for the precise approach to theologizing suggested here. Let us recall his claim that God's activity must be "visible" and involve a "progressive movement of black life." We must also note his view of a black eschatology and its essential elements. It must endorse a hope to be redeemed in the earthly life span of the oppressed. These principles suggest that a comparison of the future black situation with the present must evince tangible differences in the direction of the amelioration of black misery—if, in fact, reality has the structures Jones presupposes in his theology of hope. I am simply asking that he identify the features of human history, especially black history with its surplus of suffering, where he is willing to say that this is the ground for black hope. And it must be kept in mind that he does not assert that hope is an arbitrary leap of faith; rather, he seemingly accepts the view that hope is a faith interpretation of some actual event.

In studying Jones's materials and trying to classify them, I find it necessary to differentiate between an *ontology* of hope and a *psychology* of hope. The former concludes that there is a basis for hope because reality has a definite structure. In this context, for instance, it could be argued that a black theology of hope is feasible if it can be shown that God is benevolent, powerful, and not racist. This approach demands a specific validation procedure, a particular method of theologizing. It isolates and illuminates the crucial experiences that substantiate that these structures of reality are in fact there. In short, ontological analysis and ontological validation are necessary.

A psychology of hope, however, does not require ontological analysis or validation. The need here is to distinguish between those beliefs which inspire hope and those which lead to despair or indifference. Accordingly, the principal object of analysis is not reality per se but the belief systems of a worshiping community. The theological enterprise here is completed, once a complex of beliefs with a high coefficient of hope has been formulated. Determining the connection between the beliefs and reality or ontology is at best a theological luxury.

Though Jones and other black theologians apparently aim at an ontology of hope, what they in fact produce should be labeled a psychology of hope. By making this distinction we necessarily accent their failure to engage in ontological validation. It would be remiss if attention were not called to the crucial issue that Jones and J. Deotis Roberts, in particular, raise by their approach to the matter, and that is, should a theodicy for the oppressed be a *psychology* or an *ontology* of hope? I am convinced that this is the future issue of import for black theology.

It is not my intention to eliminate the category of hope from black theology. Hope is necessary to motivate an oppressed people to undertake its liberation. What I insist upon is some clarity about the different types of hope. Must a black theology appeal primarily to an extrahuman or suprahuman ground? Is hope in God, as they interpret him, the only basis for black religion? If this is what black theologians affirm, then they are obliged to justify hope in this suprahuman factor in light of the intolerable surplus of black suffering, which is their own point of departure for theologizing. If they invoke God as their hope, they had better be certain that He is in fact on the side of black people. For my part, I would emphasize an *anthropology* of hope rather than a *theology* of hope. By this I express a conviction not to seek aid beyond the human level.

Theologizing from the Black Perspective

An examination of the issue of divine racism is also required by the *de novo* approach implicit in Jones's system. Several pointers disclose that this is his way of executing the theological enterprise. There is first the recognition of the necessity of theologizing from the black perspective. He acknowledges that the black theologian must move the theological furniture around in a manner quite different from traditional Christian and contemporary white theologians:

> The traditional content of systematic theology may well not correspond to that of much of the literature of black theology. Black theology . . . may not be as concerned to describe such traditional themes as the eternal nature of God's existence. . . . Much of the task of black theology is to reclaim a people from humiliation, and in the process of so doing, it may well neglect such unrelated subjects as humility before man and guilt before God.[15]

What is this to say but that the norm for selecting and rejecting from the theological tradition is discovered in the necessities of black liberation? The principle affirmed here is that the black theologian should not desire or expect to fit black theology into the customary Christian or biblical mold. Rather, he should determine whether the biblical faith and the Christian tradition fit the needs of black liberation. My concern is not to urge blacks to abandon Christianity and the Bible. For the moment, I leave it an open question whether black liberation and Christian faith are soul brothers, distant cousins, unrelated, or archenemies.

Jones also approvingly cites Geddes Hanson's description of the task of black theology. And one can hardly deny that this account pressures blacks to theologize without constantly looking over their shoulders at a tradition they have already labeled racist in parts:

> It has become obvious to many blacks that the time has come to insist on the inadequacy of any theology that presumes to relate the fact of God to the facts of human life without accepting the peculiarities of black life as data. Black theology brings its reflections on black experience to the theological conference table claiming itself to be the salt without which any attempt to do theological business in America today is without savor.
>
> Implicit in the previous remarks are the assumptions that Black theology, in doing its job well, will force Protestant theology to the point of reconsidering its eschatology, its ecclesiology and its anthropology. It must in fact do more.[16]

Hanson is arguing here that the black perspective must be afforded coequal and co-ordinate theological importance and truth; and most important, this is the status the black theologian himself must give his craft. Accordingly, black theology cannot at the outset assume the prior importance or inherent truth of traditional theology. Indeed it contradicts itself as *black* theology if prior value, rather than disvalue, is assigned to the tradition, for the precondition for doing a black theology is the conclusion that there is an unacknowledged white theology that must be modified, supplemented, or replaced.

I also understand Hanson, and Jones through him, to say that the test of the success of a black theology is the degree to which it compels Christian theologians to rethink, recast, and refurbish their faith claims. This can hardly be accomplished if the black theologian annexes these claims, prior to the necessary theological housecleaning.

A primary reason for raising the question, Is God a white racist? is to force the black theologian to consider *every* theological category in his arsenal, and in the whole biblical and Christian tradition, in terms of its support for oppression. This is the import of the *de novo* approach described here. In fact it seems necessary to ask whether any black theology is authentically black if it does not incorporate this theological approach.

I wonder, after the analysis of Jones and Roberts (whom I discuss next) if they have not placed too much emphasis on the present belief system of a certain segment of black worshipers, regarding its alleged essentials as unexpendable. They presuppose that black theology must honor these beliefs, and thus certain concepts such as goodness of God are not challenged. The black theologian, I maintain, must be bold and audacious; he must conduct a comprehensive appraisal of the tradition to determine its liberation coefficient. He must initiate a theological audit of the entire tradition, adding to it or reducing it in terms of his perspective and his needs—but never making his perspective "the truth." If his inspection is not exhaustive, if he does not critically examine even the most basic tenet, e.g. God's benevolence, if he begins his examination with an a priori conclusion about the oppressive or non-oppressive factor of specific categories, the cause of black liberation may well suffer. I advance this thesis for further examination: Does our oppression result from our failure to make an all-inclusive survey of the tradition from the black perspective? To ask about God's character relative to blacks, about his possible racist leanings, is no more and no less than to initiate this undertaking.

X

J. DEOTIS ROBERTS:
A PSYCHOLOGY OF BLACK LIBERATION

Roberts defines his position in conscious opposition to the theology of Cone and Cleage. It will become obvious, however, that though they are theological opponents on certain issues—the Christian status of violence is one—their theodicies evince the same question-begging errors and problems.

To understand the inner logic of Roberts' treatment of black suffering, it is necessary to consider the theological norms that control his interpretive framework. Uppermost in this respect is identifying the actual criteria he employs to determine the authenticity, or "soul" quality, of theological concepts. Two components constitute his yardstick: First, a theological category is authentic only if it allows for the co-ordinate rank of liberation and reconciliation as theological goals, and honors the demands of each. Since these twin goals also describe Roberts' understanding of the core of Christian faith, they also determine the Christian character of a given theological position.

There is a second norm, which is easy to identify but more difficult to label: the psychological, or perhaps more accurately, the psychoreligious needs of an oppressed group as these are expressed in specific theological beliefs. The following statements illustrate the intended norm. "Against the consciousness of unjust treatment, an unloving relationship based on racism, . . . there is a need to believe that God is just, loving and merciful. . . ."[1] In the same vein, Roberts argues that black theology must adopt "the theological interpretation of evil [that] will bring comfort and assurance to black people. . . ."[2] Roberts is asserting in these statements that victims of racism require a special concept of God if their life is to be meaningful and not collapse into debilitating despair and quietism. This emphasis upon the psychoreligious assurance or homeostatic quality of theological concepts is present throughout Roberts' thought.

It is important to note that the psychoreligious units Roberts places at the center of his system turn out to be miniature theodicies. Each involves an affirmation of God's intrinsic goodness, and each implies that God is not a white racist. The experiences that constitute oppression are likely counterevidence to Roberts' faith claims. Over against these, Roberts places a complex of assurance-producing categories, which have the effect of nullifying the counterevidential quality of oppression. In this way, Roberts is able to maintain the original faith claim of God's intrinsic goodness.

That psychological weight is given top rank is also supported by less explicit evidence. Where we encounter a concept that, according to Roberts, expresses "good psychology" but "bad theology,"[3] he accepts it as authentic. On the other hand, where the concept is "bad psychology" but "good theology,"[4] he rejects it.

Thus Roberts' psychological norm reduces to this methodological principle: theological positions must be evaluated in terms of their comfort, or homeostatic, quotient. It is also worth noting that the effect of this norm is to tie black theology to the present belief system of black religion, rather than serving as its essential critic. Roberts' implicit argument that black theology must conform to the psychological needs and beliefs of black worshipers today is a crucial issue for a black theology of liberation, which demands a short excursus at this juncture.

Psychological Security or Liberating Impact

It is my contention that the psychological norm should not have the rank that Roberts and others give it. I would place the proliberation quotient, i.e. the capacity to exterminate oppression, above the ability to satisfy psychological needs. This is not to deny the importance of the latter but only its supremacy.

The issue at stake here can be put in other terms: Do all beliefs with a high assurance component also possess a high liberation factor? Apparently not, as Mays's discussion in *The Negro's God* illustrates. He describes a variant of the "whole world in His hand" concept, which provides psychological security and hope but is, at the same time, highly "compensatory," an adjective Mays uses for "counterrevolutionary":

If death comes to you, it comes because God permits it, and if God permits it, you ought to take a Christian view of the situation. If God permits it to come to you, just say, "I am no better than anybody else." We ought not to set ourselves against God and say God has not done justice by us.

The implication here seems to be that God permits everything to happen that does happen and there is nothing man can do about it. Things could not happen if God did not permit them to happen. That belief . . . goes a long way in helping people to adjust themselves to the inevitable. However painful and heart-rending the death of mother may be, the load is perhaps easier to carry if that person believes that it was God's will. Even though the idea may be false, it has great value for the person who believes it. . . . It [also] has the tendency to lead one to take a complacent, laissez-faire attitude toward life in that the person sees the will of God in all that happens.[5]

The point must not be overlooked that Roberts himself ranks the liberation factor above the psychological component in sev-

eral instances. It is admitted that not every unit in the belief
system of black religion should be affirmed; rather, certain concepts must be dumped if liberation is to become a reality. Roberts also allows that though certain aspects of the slave theology had a significant homeostatic and survival value, such
as "the pie in the sky eschatology," they are no longer adequate
for black life today. These concepts are to be abandoned, not
because they no longer provide comfort for blacks today but
because they endanger the goal of black liberation.

But once it is allowed that the psychological and the liberation factors do not always coincide—and this is the single
premise I wish to affirm at this point—the black theologian is
forced into a fundamental choice. It is obvious, in my view,
how the choice should be made.

Mays's description points to another related issue: the concept of God's sovereignty and its capacity to instill a sense of
security and comfort to the oppressed. The passage just cited
expressed the consolation inherent in the belief that God permits all that happens in human history. This belief can provide
assurance only because it presupposes God's intrinsic goodness.
As long as the world is in the hands of a benevolent deity,
human affairs are "in good hands," even if one is a slave. The
import for theodicy is obvious: all that happens is therefore
a good and an aspect of God's essential plan. Accordingly, corrective activity is not entertained or undertaken. The end result,
in sum, is quietism.

The counterliberation factor here is so prominent that there
can be little question of the black theologians' rejection. But
it is precisely at this point that the thorny problem arises. Once
God's absolute sovereignty, as described by Mays, is removed,
how are we then to draw the boundaries where His sovereign
will still extends and where the contrary or co-operative will
of man is exercised? This question is crucial, for it involves
the decision where we should submit to suffering and where
we should seek its elimination.

Moreover, some special criteriology is required here. The
difficulty of formulating this measuring tool has already been

noted. We need only recall Panaloux's agony as he tried to decide whether it was permissible for a priest to call a doctor. The black theologian should sense the same dilemma immediately if he is forced to answer a similar question without recourse to question-begging devices: Should a black Christian call a doctor? Should a black Christian seek to eliminate his poverty?[6]

A third issue concludes the excursus: Should or can there be a single black theology that attempts to speak to all segments of the black community in an authoritative way, or should we accept the principle of "different theological strokes for different black folk"? I start with the conclusion that one man's psychological cup of tea is another's poison. Accordingly I would strenuously object to the argument that only Christian theism can be the foundation for black hope.

None of the extant black theologies, in my view, has the breadth to span the spectrum of black religion and encompass the generational differences in the black community. They speak primarily to and for those who are already committed theists and Christians. I sense, however, the growth of a more humanistic religion, manifest in part in the black power movement,[7] with entirely different psychological and religious needs. A black theology with the pantheological and transgenerational capacity to be the single voice for black religion has not yet emerged—if it ever will.

Black theology will require different black theologies of hope, some of which will affirm concepts that from the perspective of the available black theologies may only lead to black despair, e.g. where there is no assertion of a future reality after death. But when we consider that the contemporary black theologians seem to ground their hope in a God who has not yet been shown to be the champion of black people, cannot their systems also be regarded as counsels of despair?

I would also suggest that Roberts and others place too much emphasis upon black religion as "survival" religion, and this leads to an inevitable de-emphasis of its liberation impact. I grant that survival has its legitimate, its necessary place and role. It is obviously a necessary condition for liberation or anything else. I would also acknowledge that during certain periods, such as slavery, survival was by far the more pressing need than liberation. What I object to is the continuation of a survival model that in today's context may be anachronistic, especially if this model is defended on the grounds of its survival value for previous generations. The value of a theological category, I submit, should be gauged in terms of its liberation coefficient for the present and future, rather than its psychological comfort for a past, or even the present, generation. It would also appear that the black theologians themselves are committed to the same conclusion, once they define their systems as theologies of liberation.

The Issue of Divine Racism in Roberts' System

Thus far we have focused on Roberts' theological norm because of its importance for his analysis of black suffering. The concern now is to show that central aspects of Roberts' own stated methodology introduce the issue of divine racism, an issue, however, that he does not explicitly consider or refute. Without this analysis and refutation of divine racism, his system involves an inherent inconsistency.

It is easy to show that the fundamental pillars of his thought involve an implicit denial that God is a white racist. Liberation and reconciliation presuppose a God who is for all men and their well-being. These concerns, in Roberts' thought, cannot be the activities of a racist God. In addition, his identification of "the God of the Exodus" as "the black man's God,"[8] as one who delivers the oppressed from bondage, presupposes the same denial.

The present purpose, however, aims at a different demonstration: to show that Roberts advances the same complex of concepts that raise the issue of divine racism. In this connection, it will be evident that he accepts the essentials of the concept of ethnic suffering and also the necessity of the counterevidential method in black theology.

An earlier argument established that the counterevidence method requires a framework capable of accommodating the evidence that appears to contradict the position being defended. In Roberts' context, this reduces to the validation of a particular doctrine of God in the light of its contrary evidence, black suffering as ethnic suffering. "The moral attributes of God," he argues, "in reference to the real experiences of evil and suffering are of primary interest to Black Christians. . . . The essential question for Black Christians is not: Does God exist? It is rather: Does God care?"[9] Thus it is to be expected that "the Christian understanding of God must develop out of the black presence in a white racist society, and out of an experience of oppression endured for almost four centuries."[10]

There can be little doubt that the following passage when joined to the previous citations affirms the essential features of ethnic suffering: maldistribution, negative quality of suffering, enormity, and non-catastrophic character:

Why such an unequal distribution when the One in charge is not only all-loving but all-wise as well . . . ? We have made the point repeatedly that black people are no better and no worse than whites; therefore any explanation that does not make understandable the unequal distribution of suffering in the black experience is not helpful to black people.[11]

In these passages Roberts is asserting that we can reach a trustworthy conclusion about God's moral attributes only by donning the spectacles of black oppression, with its inequality of suffering, and viewing God through them. The claim that God cares for blacks, in short, must accommodate the counterevidence, four centuries of oppression. Is there any doubt that Roberts here commits himself, and black theology in turn, to the counterevidential approach?

It also appears that Roberts asserts the principle that God is the sum of His acts, along with its focus upon the present and past acts of God:

Instead of moving from the future to the present, we

move from the present to the future—at least to begin. Only after we are aware of what God is doing in this world to make life more human for blacks may we speak of God's future breaking into our present and look forward to the new age.[12]

Given Roberts' explicit assertion of the key concepts that raise the issue of divine racism, the question immediately arises: Why does he bypass the issue of divine racism? The simple explanation is that he chooses at the outset to utilize only those theological options which define God as intrinsically benevolent. As he says, "We assume that God exists and that he is a benevolent providential God."[13] That this affirmation is assumed is also supported by the absence of any sustained argument to account for black suffering in the light of God's benevolence.

At this juncture, the issue of Roberts' internal consistency can be raised relative to his methodology. His stated method affirms that we must plumb black oppression to see what it implies, *before* we can reach definitive conclusions about God's moral character and His caring for all men. In this way, black suffering becomes the normative interpretive box into which God's caring must be fitted, if it can be fitted at all.

His actual method, however, starts with the prior assumption of God's intrinsic goodness, and he then seeks to fit black suffering into that framework. In this way, God's assumed benevolence, rather than the black experience, forms the perimeter into which black suffering must be assimilated.

We may reach the same conclusion in another way: Having first argued for a concept of God that starts with four centuries of black oppression and having made the inequality of black suffering the crucial feature that an authentic concept of God must assimilate, how can he make the benevolence of God the point of departure for analyzing that suffering? Surely this is to put the cart before the horse, and Dr. Roberts is plunged into a clear self-contradiction.

We do not have to look far to discover why Roberts starts

with the prior assumption of God's benevolence. The answer lies in his concern for the psychological needs of the oppressed blacks. "We need to know," he concludes, "that there is no evil in the nature of God; that all evil is external to him. We need the assurance that this God is not capricious or arbitrary in the exercise of his will or power, and that he is benevolent and morally upright."[14] In an even more explicit statement, we find him willing to endorse Panaloux's ultimate solution—the leap of love—in spite of its inherent dangers. Roberts resolves to believe and to act as if ultimate reality were intrinsically good, notwithstanding the counterevidence:

> A black theology must somehow maintain trust in the absolute goodness and omnipotence of God notwithstanding the fact of moral evil, . . . against which we must struggle. We must confront evil and find through the resources of our faith the wherewithal to stand up to life.[15]

Another question can be put to Roberts that illuminates his question-begging treatment of the issue of divine racism. Can he legitimately exclude without consideration one of the principal interpretations implied by the very materials he himself establishes as crucial? His approach formulates a universe of discourse that excludes at the beginning alternative interpretations of four centuries of black suffering, e.g. divine racism.

His stated method and point of departure make the question, Does God care? a live question. His answer, however, denatures the question. He answers the question, in essence, by arguing that a negative response cannot be countenanced, because of its unsettling psychological consequences. This approach may well be appropriate for a psychology of hope, but hardly for an ontology of hope.

Roberts' Critique of Traditional Theodicies

Roberts, like Cone, explicitly rejects several explanations of black suffering as incompatible with the needs and demands of black theology. This taking of a position creates severe problems for the internal consistency of Roberts' system and delimits the available options for his own personal statement of theodicy. Of critical importance in this respect is his unreliable refutation of the theodicy of deserved punishment.

In his critique of traditional theodicies Roberts is guided by the rationale of guarding two indispensable theological claims: God's intrinsic goodness and the undeserved character of black suffering. Roberts recognizes that to establish that black suffering is not merited, he is obliged to refute the claim that it is deserved punishment. The theodicy of deserved punishment, he summarizes, must be scrapped, because it cannot account for the unequal and inexact distribution of suffering in general and black suffering in particular. We all recognize, according to Roberts, that "the outright wicked man gets along so well in this life," and "often the best people we know endure too much suffering."[16] And since "blacks are no better and no worse than whites," a surplus of black suffering remains an enigma in the context of deserved punishment or an interpretation of suffering as disciplinary.

It is obvious that Roberts begs the question here. Note his conclusion that "blacks are no better and no worse than whites." But in the framework of a theodicy of deserved punishment, this is precisely what has to be proved, not assumed. His statement assumes, but does not substantiate, that blacks are no worse than whites.

Another point must be made regarding Roberts' refutation of the theodicy of deserved punishment. We must give proper weight to the fact that Roberts actually attempts to demonstrate two propositions that must be separated. He aims at the general conclusion that black suffering is *undeserved*. But he also seeks to establish that black suffering is not the consequence of or an expression of *divine disfavor*. However, to validate the first in no way confirms the second. It is precisely at this point that the interpretation of divine racism must be considered. It would support the conclusion that black suffering is an expression of divine disfavor but would not entail the view that black suffering is deserved punishment. By collapsing divine disfavor and deserved punishment into the same theological package and criticizing only the latter, he begs the question regarding the former.

Another inconsistency must be pinpointed: We note Roberts' use of the inequality of black suffering as a polemical device. He insists that if a theodicy—here the theodicy of deserved punishment—cannot explain disproportionate black suffering, then its credentials as an authentic theodicy must be withdrawn. But how can he criticize the theodicy of deserved punishment in this way without seeing that his own approach is also vulnerable to the very same challenge? Let us apply the same challenge to Roberts' approach of beginning with the assumption of God's intrinsic goodness. The consequence is obvious. Roberts does not have to accommodate the very materials he concludes are unassimilable in the theodicy of deserved punishment, because he establishes rules that allow him to proceed without consideration of the counterevidence. If Roberts' method were applied to his own system, surely it would collapse like a house of cards. In actuality, the real consequence of his approach, postulating God's benevolence without giving full weight to the counterevidence, is to eliminate all legitimate grounds for refuting any theodicy he thinks is defective.

We must also pinpoint another instance where Roberts, in order to refute an opposing theodicy, incorporates a principle that he does not permit to be used against himself: Consider his view that the "wicked thrive in this life." The effect of this emphasis is to eliminate the other world as the place where justice is meted out equally. His own theodicy, however, wants to honor the principle of a future beyond this life, because it is psychologically necessary for an oppressed people. But if the "in this life" norm is replaced by the "in the next life" regarding the fortunes of the wicked, his "refutation" of the theodicy of deserved punishment is severely damaged. Now the arena of ultimate rewards and punishments is no longer this life, but the next. There the wicked will receive their just deserts, and thus there is no inequality of suffering in the first place. The theodicy of deserved punishment stands unblemished.

If this analysis is correct, Roberts has refuted the position of merited punishment only by refusing his opponent the precise principle he himself makes normative. His own principles demonstrate that his rebuttal of the theodicy of deserved punishment is fallacious.

Roberts' Theodicy and Divine Racism

Having considered the theodicies Roberts rejects, it is necessary to move to a discussion of his own personal statement of theodicy. His position is an admixture of the following features: an affirmation of God's omnibenevolence and omnipotence, aspects of the "beyond human comprehension" theodicy of Job, a modification of the theodicy of redemptive suffering already analyzed in the discussion of Washington, and a doctrine of eschatology that is both "realized" and "unrealized."

The purpose here is to show that this complex of positions, when joined with the theodicies he rejects, reintroduces rather than removes the charge of divine racism.

A black theodicy, Roberts concludes, must affirm both the omnipotence and the omnibenevolence of God. His rationale is clearly the psychological needs of the oppressed. If either the goodness or the power of God is questioned, black hope collapses into despair:

Black theology . . . must hold to the all-goodness and all-power of God . . . out of sheer necessity.[17]

The concept of an impotent God is not very appealing to a people seeking Black power for determining their own destiny. What is needed to inspire faith in the oppressed under the sustained domination of the oppressor is belief in a God of all-power who is able to promise the ultimate vindication of the good and the defeat of evil and injustice.[18]

At other points, God's omnipotence is translated into His sovereignty over human history. "God is not only a creator-spirit, a loving father, he is lord of history as well. As a provident God he has deposited a controlling purpose in history that promises to be fulfilled."[19]

Once Roberts has defined God's nature and His relation to human history in this way, try as he might, the issue of divine racism must inevitably surface. The other parts of his theodicy can be considered as escape routes from this conclusion, but each turns out to be a theological dead end. Roberts' doctrine of God, along with his view of ethnic suffering, puts him in a theological corner from which he does not extricate himself.

His appeal to the theodicy of the Book of Job does not solve his problem. The core of Job's view, in his interpretation, is a concept of God "whose ways are past finding out." I would regard this strategy as a variant of the "beyond human comprehension" theodicy. A radically different or wholly other relation is affirmed between God and man relative to specific categories, such as power and wisdom. It has already been established that this approach does not, however, refute the accusation of divine racism but in fact provides the logical and theological backdrop for it.

The failure of the "beyond human comprehension" theodicy is not critical for Roberts, since he assigns only provisional merit to Job's resolution, noting on the one hand that it "is no longer very comforting,"[20] and on the other that a theodicy close to the heart of Christian faith must move in the direction of a theodicy of redemptive suffering.

A theodicy of redemptive suffering, however, also leaves Roberts' problem unresolved. The dangers of this strategy have already been outlined sufficiently in the discussion of Washington. Though Roberts modifies Washington's specific viewpoint, the core of the latter's thought is retained intact. Acknowledging that Washington's theodicy "has real possibilities," that it has "a firm stand within the Judaeo-Christian tradition," and that it "provides the historical and sociological context in which Black theology must treat the symbolism of the suffering servant," Roberts criticizes it because it gives insufficient weight to Jesus Christ and the Church as the suffering servant / chosen people. He also insists that the black theologian should carefully inspect the history of Jewish suffering for its important insights on ethnic suffering and theodicy. But none of this moves him far from the central conclusion of Washington, which also informs his own position: "The black experience of suffering is related to the Biblical message of redemptive suffering."[21] Here again we are facing the crucial issue already considered: Do we beg the question if we classify blacks as the suffering servant prior to the definitive liberation event?

It is interesting, though fatal to his own argument, that Roberts seems to emphasize the two events of suffering and exaltation-liberation as defining for the suffering servant. Consider the following passage, with its unmistakable accent upon the problem of assimilating the enormity and inequality of black suffering into the hypothesis of redemptive suffering and the conclusion that affirmative interpretations of suffering are questionable from the black perspective, particularly if they involve *future* suffering for blacks. Roberts' emphasis, in short, is upon the cessation of black suffering regardless of an alleged higher purpose it may serve. We will see shortly that other passages, as well as his doctrine of realized eschatology, lead to the same conclusion.

> Many blacks are turned off by the idea that their suffering as a people may have some purpose. Even as a theologian who has searched for meaning in the concept of redemptive suffering, my emotions recoil at the idea of further suffering for blacks, even if that suffering may be fruitful in the end. Whenever someone makes the suggestion that perhaps the clue to the black man's chosenness is his suffering, my mind raises real questions. Is it necessary that such oppression and undeserved suffering continue in order that grace may abound? My suspicion is further aroused by the fact that the affirmative attitude comes from the side of the oppressor and not from the

oppressed themselves.[22] This leads me to suggest that whatever understanding of our chosenness emerges in a Black theology must take under serious account the fact that the black man's experience has been purged in the fires of suffering. But our interpretation of chosenness must . . . hold up the promise of a better day.[23]

To carry Roberts' argument one step further, the theological hypothesis of redemptive suffering cannot account for the *totality* of black suffering in the past: "In the white racist society, which is America, blacks have borne a constant cross for more than four centuries. All suffering has not, by any means, been an act of God; neither has it been redemptive suffering."[24]

Here Roberts insists that black theology must make an unambiguous distinction between redemptive and non-redemptive suffering, and that blacks should endure the former but annihilate the latter. "Much that we have undergone has been a result of 'man's inhumanity to man' and does not arise out of a Christian understanding of God's providence. This is the cross of our experience that we must get rid of." In other words, to be legitimate, the strategy of redemptive suffering must lead ultimately to its own destruction. "At the same time we use suffering creatively and redemptively, we must seek to render it unnecessary as a way of life."[25]

By dichotomizing between redemptive and non-redemptive suffering, Roberts seeks to remove responsibility for the totality of black suffering from God's hands. But this strategy is successful only if Roberts provides the indispensable criterion for differentiating between the two. Without this criteriology we cannot determine where God's responsibility ends and man's guilt begins. Nor can we decide what suffering is to be endured and what is not.

Moreover, in the context of divine racism, the failure to provide this criteriology is tantamount to begging the question. It removes the onus for the *surplus* of black suffering from God and shifts it to man. But Roberts' doctrine of God's omnipotence and sovereignty over human history places God in the docket regarding this surplus, and He must remain there until Roberts tells us precisely what instances of black suffering should be traced to God, that is, are redemptive. His strategy here is useless without the criteriology it presupposes. Indeed, without it, having traced part of black suffering to God Himself, the interpretation of divine racism again surfaces.

The identical issue arises again when Roberts concludes, "The black Christian needs to have clearly presented the distinction between man's disorder and God's design."[26] Agreed, this distinction is indeed crucial, but Roberts does not tell us how to make it. In point of fact, none of the black theologians does! But having indicated the necessity of this criteriology, Roberts is faced with the equally menacing question of how to develop the formula for separating redemptive from non-redemptive suffering. Are there specific sufferings that fall neatly into one class or the other? We should recall in this connection that blacks, at one time or another, have labeled nearly every suffering, including slavery, redemptive. To make the problem even more complicated and immune to a ready solution, it must be recalled that the precondition for redemptive suffering is the innocence of the sufferer. The distinction between redemptive and non-redemptive suffering, in short, must be accompanied by a persuasive demonstration that the suffering in question is not deserved. In Roberts' specific case, the weakness of his critique of the theodicy of deserved punishment leaves this necessary condition unfulfilled.

Roberts' Eschatology: Realized or Unrealized?

Roberts' theodicy is incomplete without a discussion of his eschatology. But here a crucial interpretive problem arises. There appears to be a basic ambiguity in his eschatological position, and this makes it difficult to identify and describe his definitive position. My analysis, therefore, reduces to a description of the two basic positions that can be unearthed, with the view in mind of raising the specific questions and issues that Roberts' subsequent response might clarify.

"Eschatology for blacks," Roberts affirms, "must be both realized and unrealized."[27] I will argue that his description of realized eschatology leaves us with a muddy picture of unrealized eschatology and an even less clear picture of how both are correlated with his general position in theodicy.

Roberts defines realized eschatology as "the manifestation of the will of God in the present, *abstractly* as social justice and *concretely* as goods and services to 'humanize' life."[28] Apparently he is arguing here that black hope in the future must be based upon an actual improvement of the present black situation i.e. socially and economically. A black theology must be a "'realizable eschatology' in the here and now, in order to be hopeful to blacks. The theme of 'the waiting God' is unacceptable for those who have been waiting so long and who are tired of waiting, . . . The 'I am of God' is more impressive than the 'I will be of God.'"[29]

His criticism of Rubem Alves makes the same point. He accuses Alves of being "too futuristic" and admonishes black theologians to be more "concerned about their present," for unless something happens in the present, there will be little to hope for in the future—at least in this life."[30] Here again we find the emphasis upon concrete events of black liberation in the present.

The principle of realized eschatology also informs Roberts' doctrine of God, especially the understanding of God's activity in the future. All that we can say about the God of the future is contingent upon our affirmations about His present and past activity. Roberts is explicit on this point, and here he affirms, as elsewhere, the principle of God as the sum of his acts:

> Instead of moving from the future to the present, we move from the present to the future, at least to begin. Only after we are aware of what God is doing in this world to make life more human for blacks may we speak of God's future breaking into our present and look forward to the new age.[31]

The same applies to any doctrine that points to the ultimate consummation of the divine purpose in creation and history. In sum, the clue to God's purpose for creation and human history, the key to unraveling His moral character, is the character of His present and past activity in black history.

Roberts' interpretation of realized eschatology creates a number of problems for the clarity and consistency of his theodicy. His view of realized eschatology pushes him to identify concrete events of black improvement or liberation in the present. But it is precisely at this point that the inequality of black suffering—Roberts' starting point—wrecks his argument. This is the same error that plagued Major Jones. The inequality of black suffering excludes the very events required to establish that God cares for blacks. Moreover, Roberts' own emphasis upon the "present manifestation" of God's purpose also limits the importation of past occurrences, such as the Exodus or the Cross-Resurrection, unless they, too, are made contemporaneous and actualized in the present as concrete events of black liberation.

The maldistribution of black suffering suggests that if black hope in the future is to be something other than wishful thinking, God's activity relative to blacks—or, what amounts to the same thing, His activity relative to whites—must be radically different. If this is accurate, two questions face us: Can a concept of realized eschatology accommodate a radical shift in God's behavior or the character of human existence? Roberts, it seems, is caught in a logical noose. His concept of realized eschatology reduces God's future activity to the character of His present actions; God's future deeds would be in some sense the continuation of, or at least similar to, His present conduct. Yet the present maldistribution of black suffering suggests that God must perform in an almost "wholly other" fashion to effect black liberation.

In this connection it is necessary to ask, Where is the basis in the present for blacks to hope that God's activity will be different? Indeed, if we are to emphasize the similarity and continuity between God's present and future deeds vis-à-vis blacks, the interpretation that He is indifferent or hostile to blacks seems more promising and consistent. It appears that Roberts is grounding his hope not on the concrete events his stated position requires, but upon his prior assumption of God's benevolence—notwithstanding evidence to the contrary.

The issue also boils down to deciding which theodicies can accommodate the type of radical shift in human fortune and divine conduct Roberts anticipates. A theodicy of redemptive suffering is a likely candidate, for it permits the sweeping metamorphosis, the shift from humiliation to exaltation, from last to first. But as we saw in the previous discussion, this theodicy is not available to Roberts.

Certain interpretations of unrealized eschatology, i.e. what God will do in the future, also sanction a radical change in the character of man's existence. This is true in particular of an apocalyptic viewpoint, which sees the future as a radical transformation of the present. Roberts rejects this view, however, which leads one to ask if his concept of realized eschatology, with its emphasis upon "present manifestation," leaves any room at all for a theory of unrealized eschatology. A general discussion of the ambiguity between these two poles of his eschatology is required at this juncture:

I conclude that Roberts' view of realized eschatology commits him to identify some definitive event of salvation that, if not unrepeatable, is at least unsurpassable. I would contend as well that the relation between the event(s) of realized eschatology and those which follow is that of essential similarity. What is to be excluded is the type of movement that begins with humiliation and arrives at exaltation. To specify the "yet to come" as dissimilar to "what is," i.e. the consequence of the event of realized eschatology, is simply to challenge the latter's ultimacy. Can one make the poles of unrealized and realized eschatology coequal without forcing the question, Has the definitive event of salvation in fact occurred? The more Roberts accents God's redemptive activity in the present or past, such as the Cross-Resurrection, the more superfluous it is to speak of unrealized eschatology. Indeed, it seems that the unequal distribution of black suffering calls into question either the definitive or the universal character of the Cross-Resurrection. If in Christ humiliation and exaltation are combined, what are the tangible events in the lives of blacks that manifest that the Resurrection has in fact occurred in power? If the surplus of black suffering still persists after the alleged event of God's "victory," how then are we to regard the Cross-Resurrection in view of Roberts' description of it and its consequences for black theology?

> For the most part, black Christians take the historicity of the resurrection with all seriousness. So much depends upon the resurrection and its power. . . . To black Christians the resurrection has much to say about God's direction of human affairs. It reveals God's providence as well as his salvific work among men. A righteous, just, merciful, loving, powerful God still runs history. At the cross evil at its worst confronted holiness at its best, and love won the victory over hate. . . . Because of resurrection power, life has triumphed over death. . . . A new age has come into being, God's new age. The climax of a struggle for justice and righteousness in history has occurred and the victory belongs to God. . . . The resurrection is the basis of a black hope secure in the God of the resurrection, who is a God of love and power, who promises to be with us always and to make all things new.[32]

I would simply ask Roberts to square the foregoing account of the Resurrection with the surplus of black suffering he so poignantly describes.

Two lines of argumentation are open to Roberts here: He could follow the example of Jewish theology and challenge the decisive character and salvific singularity of the Resurrection. That is, the Resurrection may be an important occurrence in man's salvation history, but the conditions in the alleged New Age suggest that the Messiah is yet to come. We do not have realized eschatology yet. Good theology but bad psychology?

Another option would retain the decisive aspect of the

Resurrection but question whether blacks are the intended recipients of its saving grace. This approach frontally challenges the universality of the Resurrection. Roberts has argued that the superfluity of black suffering nullifies the theodicy of deserved punishment. What theological principle prevents this conclusion: the same surplus makes problematical the universality and/or the definitive character of the Resurrection—except the assumption of God's intrinsic and universal benevolence?

To put the same issue in methodological terms will return us to an earlier discussion. Does Roberts' account of unrealized eschatology permit him to start with the assumption of God's goodness? The fact that he postulates the necessity of an unrealized eschatology can only mean that something is unsavory in the present black situation. It requires radical amelioration. And if we must look to a different relation between God and blacks, if we must look in the direction of a more benevolent and caring relation, is it not gratuitous of Roberts to make his point of departure a premise that still awaits confirmation?

Other aspects of his concept of unrealized eschatology also require clarification. He identifies several ways of interpreting this concept, but he fails to identify clearly which position is his own. For instance, is unrealized eschatology "the continuation of the best" of our this-worldly existence, or is it "a fulfillment of desires unfilled in this life"?[33] Does unrealized eschatology simply top off the process of humanization initiated by the event of realized eschatology, or does the unrealized eschatology make a decisive break? Where does Roberts want to locate the definitive event of black salvation, in the sphere of realized or of unrealized eschatology or partly in each? Can it consistently be located in both?

In light of the foregoing analysis, my summary can be brief: In reading Roberts, I sense the same error that was detected in Major Jones. Roberts indicates what theological categories correlate with a specific need arising from the oppressed condition; this boils down to the conclusion that God is on the side of the oppressed and with power. But he never validates that the universe has this character. Though he argues for the theological priority of the "combination of subjective faith and objective verification,"[34] we receive a heady dose of the former but hardly a whiff of the latter. Accordingly I conclude that the maldistribution of black suffering, which is his own starting point, remains unassimilated in his system. And in the light of his own presuppositions, the hypothesis of divine racism is not an unattractive interpretive option.

PART III

❊❊❊❊❊❊❊❊❊❊❊❊❊

Toward a Black
Theodicy for Today

XI

TOWARD A PROLEGOMENON
TO BLACK THEOLOGY

The Nature of a Prolegomenon

With the foregoing analyses as background, it is now possible to specify an aspect of my purpose that it was impossible to specify at the outset: the construction of a prolegomenon to black theology. By this, I aim at several objectives, which become clear after an analysis of the nature of a prolegomenon.

Three essential elements constitute a prolegomenon to a discipline, and these collapse into specific tasks to be executed or propositions to be demonstrated. One can identify (1) a critical or polemical feature, (2) a normative factor, and (3) a corrective or constructive objective.

The motive to undertake a prolegomenon to a discipline is the conviction that the discipline and its adherents abound in serious error. Thus the writer who proposes his study as a prolegomenon is obliged to pinpoint the inaccuracies, fallacies, and blunders that are presupposed by his critical investigation. Moreover, he is required to demonstrate that these mistakes are not peripheral but involve the very structure, the vital cogency, and the inner consistency of the system he attacks. He must establish that the error is so severe that, if uncorrected, the system will crumple like Humpty Dumpty. Nothing short of a radical reformation, nothing less than a new foundation can provide the support the system's superstructure requires.

Moreover, an effective prolegomenon must prove that the error is present not in a mere handful but in the overwhelming majority of the personnel in that discipline. Thus a cloud of disrepute hangs over their work until it is redone in the face of the new challenge advanced. In this sense, the net effect of the critical analysis is to render their conclusions untrustworthy and thus necessitate their total reappraisal in light of a new approach or perspective. A prolegomenon, then, points toward an inescapable correction and reconstruction.

The demonstration of the shortcomings of the position under attack must necessarily appeal to some standard—be it a methodological principle; a general conclusion about ultimate reality, man, suffering etc.; or a logical rule, e.g. the fallacy of begging the question. It is this yardstick that is the ultimate basis for testing, criticizing, and rejecting the positions at issue. Hence a *normative factor* is implicit in every prolegomenon.

Accordingly, the writer who intends his work as a prolegomenon must identify and justify the critical apparatus he employs.[1] For my study, this has meant the isolation of the threshold issue for black theology: the demonstration of the centrality of theodicy and the refutation of the charge of divine racism. I attempted to justify this apparatus by means of an internal analysis and criticism, establishing that it is already presupposed or explicit in the black theologies investigated. The critical apparatus, accordingly, is not an alien framework arbitrarily thrust upon their systems. If the internal criticism has been successfully executed, then any attack upon the critical apparatus of this study must also establish that this norm is *not* present, explicitly or implicitly, in the black theologies analyzed.

To review: if the critical task of the prolegomenon is carried through without substantial error, the net effect is to eliminate the available systems as accurate or comprehensive descriptions of the topic under discussion. Hence, having, as it were, cleared the field, a constructive effort is demanded to either replace or supplement the defective systems. One point must be emphasized here: Though the critical task leads toward the constructive, the two approaches should not be made correlative, like cause and effect. The difference, in sum and substance, is that of posing a question, in contrast to providing the definitive answer.

This difference is of particular importance when the prolegomenon is challenged. It should be clear that though the criticism may be faultless, the reconstruction can be totally defective. The reader should keep this distinction in mind in appraising my study, for it is the critical, Parts I and II, and not the constructive, Part III, that dominates my concern.

My own constructive enterprise, the formulation of a black theology rivaling those now available, lies in the immediate future. It will consummate in a statement utilizing the framework of "secular"[2] humanism. In fact, the purpose and content of this present book become clearer if it is seen as an attempt to make a place in the theological circle for a nontheistic model. The present work, in a real sense, is a prolegomenon to my own future statement in black theology, since the argument of this book explains why a humanistic model is necessary.

With this understanding, the reader must recognize that what follows is not my own personal statement of a black theodicy. Having demonstrated that a viable theodicy must be the foundation for contemporary black theology, my purpose now is to identify a specific type of theodicy that can serve as a blueprint for future black theologians. In this way, my task parallels that of the architect who sketches a number of possible models and not that of the contractor who builds according to one of the plans.

I advance the claim that only two models are viable for a black theodicy of liberation: secular humanism and what I call humanocentric theism. Though the essentials of the latter position will be outlined and discussed with reference to selected representatives, secular humanism is not examined. Some explanation of this omission is in order:

It has been argued, with some merit, that black religion is fundamentally theistic, and therefore any black theology that wants to be an effective handmaiden of black liberation must adopt a similar theological stance. A movement away from theism should come only if it is convincingly demonstrated that it is a hindrance to black liberation. Disregarding for the moment the issue of theological accuracy, the black theologian, for pragmatic reasons, should develop initially a theistic framework for theodicy. It is in deference to this argument that an exploration of secular humanism, my own theological position, must await another work. My concern in this book has been to identify the particular types of theism that are incompatible with a theology of liberation.

I must also confess an ulterior motive for postponing the treatment of secular humanism. I wish to identify which theistic options provide a viable framework for a theology of liberation. Humanocentric theism is such an option, and it is also the last point on the theistic spectrum before one jumps to the position of humanism. If I can demonstrate the value of humanocentric theism for a black theodicy, I have also succeeded at the same time in providing an entree for its immediate neighbor, secular humanism, into the theological arena. In this way, the discussion of humanocentric theism helps to pave the way for secular humanism as an appropriate complement for contemporary black religion.

Finally, a description of secular humanism here would carry us far beyond the proposed boundaries of the present study. I do identify and discuss briefly its constitutive feature: the functional ultimacy of man.

Essentials of a Viable Black Theodicy

Selecting a viable theodicy for black theology is no simple matter. Several demands control one's choice here. On the one hand the character of a theodicy establishes specific criteria to be honored. It must explain or account for the suffering at issue in relation to a doctrine of God or ontology. In addition, it must relate the fact of suffering and its character to a trustworthy interpretation of the nature, power, and moral quality of God and the nature of His activity in human affairs. In addition, some discussion of the nature and destiny of man, especially the interrelation of human and divine freedom, will be involved.

Since black theology defines itself as a theology of liberation or liberation-reconciliation, other demands are also influential. The liberation demand, for instance, dictates that a given theodicy must not blunt the impulse for black freedom and full humanity. More concretely, the position of quietism must be avoided. But, strictly speaking, these demands are not central to the theodicy question per se.

Since the black theologians make specific claims about the role and importance of the black church in the enterprise of liberation and about the religious and psychological sentiments of black worshipers, there are yet other factors that must be considered. With this understanding as background, it is necessary to spell out the requirements that must be uppermost in the black theologian's mind when he formulates his theodicy:

Let me say in advance that the following list is not exhaustive, nor does it express my own selection. The list, rather, is a composite of those requirements which the black theologians as a whole seem to endorse and those which emerged as central by virtue of the argument in the previous chapters. In addition, a few are generally accepted logical canons.

To repeat the general requirement already cited, a viable

black theodicy must be capable of refuting the charge of divine racism. That is to say, it must account for the features of ethnic suffering and in specified ways: (1) The refutation must not put the ultimate blame or causal responsibility at God's feet. (2) The black theologian must not simply *assume* that the charge of divine racism is false. This dictates that the rebuttal must be grounded in materials drawn from the actual black experience and not mere rational or theoretical possibilities unconnected to the actual history of blacks. (3) The refutation must not reintroduce the same charge at another level. The rebuttal of divine racism is without merit if, in the process, it leads, as for Washington, to the perpetuity of black suffering. (4) Nor can the refutation involve a comparable theological scandal: the rebuttal should not entail, for instance, the charge of divine sexism or that God is a black racist.

Other requirements are necessitated by virtue of the black theologians' concern to utilize the fundamental perspective of the Judaeo-Christian tradition in their respective formulations. In accordance therewith, (5) the framework must be theistic, more precisely, monotheistic. In addition, it must incorporate the omnipotence and benevolence of God. This means that several traditional theodicies cannot be employed; for example, dualism, two Gods in fundamental opposition, is effectively eliminated by this requirement.

The black theologians collectively reject various resolutions to the problem of black suffering, and this narrows the theological options from which a theodicy can be constructed. Accordingly, (6) a theodicy of deserved punishment cannot be employed, excepting for the moment Cleage's particular interpretation. Nor can (7) a "beyond human comprehension" theodicy. The black theologians were also hesitant to endorse any eschatological compensation for suffering experienced here and now if this meant little or no improvement in the present black condition. I interpret this to mean that (8) a viable black theology must include the possibility for the present and/or subsequent amelioration of black oppression on this side of the eschaton.

The black theologians were also unanimous in their denunciation of those positions which clearly entail quietism. Consequently, the theodicy must accommodate the radical transformation of the status quo. Stated concretely, (9) it must provide a framework for defining one's suffering as negative or oppressive. (10) It must emphasize that one's own efforts are necessary and (11) that the extermination of oppressive suffering is at least possible.

Other requirements can be lumped together under the heading of (12) commonly accepted logical canons: The explanation must be internally consistent and systematically coherent. The theodicy cannot contradict other parts of the system. I would also include here the necessity of avoiding the well-known logical fallacies, formal and informal.[3]

When we appraise the theodicies of the black theologians in the light of the foregoing requirements, each appears to be helpful and harmful in varying degrees. None fulfills every demand. Some have enormous psychological or compensatory value, because they assure the black Christian that the power of God is on his side. But they fail to rebut the charge of divine racism, and thus their psychological merit is undermined. Others harmonize well with the belief system of this generation of black worshipers but fail to honor the emerging theological instincts of the next. Finding an appropriate framework for a black theodicy for today is a bewildering dilemma. One is finally forced to ask, Is there a single theodicy that can accommodate the complex of requirements just outlined and others that the black theologians, no doubt, would add to the list?

Before a response to this inescapable and agonizing question can be attempted, it is helpful to consider the attempt of a contemporary theologian, Richard Rubenstein, to assimilate the issue of ethnic suffering within the Jewish theological tradition.[4] His analysis is especially instructive as we attempt to isolate the essentials of a viable black theodicy. First, he places the issue of ethnic suffering at the very heart of the theological enterprise. In addition, he adopts the counterevidential approach to theologizing. And his solution to the enigma of ethnic suffering is illuminating, though not particularly serviceable for a black theodicy of liberation. He finds that only a radical theology or his special variety of the death-of-God theology can effectively handle the issue of ethnic suffering.

A death-of-God theology, in my view, is not the only or even the most appropriate theological response to ethnic suffering. Thus it is necessary to show that Rubenstein's conclusion is not exhaustive. Humanocentric theism, for instance, can easily accommodate all of Rubenstein's pressing points on his theological agenda. I would make the very same claim for secular humanism, a position that Rubenstein considers, but fallaciously rejects.

Richard Rubenstein: A Jewish Theodicy

The most appropriate interpretive framework for analyzing Rubenstein's position is to regard it as a prolegomenon to contemporary Jewish theology, with the critical, normative, and constructive elements described above. His purpose is to demonstrate that Jewish theology in general and Jewish theodicy in particular are wholly inadequate. Jewish theology must be scrapped, because it does not provide a viable theodicy. Jewish theologians, he concludes, have failed to account for Auschwitz, the symbol of Jewish oppression. Thus his critical task assumes the general form of criticizing contemporary and past Jewish theologians in terms of the normative principle of Auschwitz. His constructive task seeks to replace the extant theologies rather than reform or supplement them; for instance, he replaces the traditional Judaeo-Christian theology of history with a theology of nature.

This general outline of Rubenstein's position must be complemented with a more detailed description of the normative principle of his prolegomenon and some of its methodological implications. The title of his first work, *After Auschwitz,* indicates that the watershed for Jewish theology, for him, is the horrible complex of Jewish suffering. Accordingly, it and the issues and questions it expresses constitute the threshold issue for Jewish theology. "No Jewish theology," he contends, "will possess even a remote degree of relevance to contemporary life if it ignores the question of God and the death camps. This is the question for Jewish theology in our times."[5]

Looked at methodologically, ethnic suffering establishes the theological agenda for Jewish theology; it is the necessary point of departure for theological reflection and construction. Not only does Jewish suffering raise the fundamental question for the Jewish theologian, it also provides the definitive answer. For Rubenstein, what the theologian can legitimately assert about the nature of God and man is dictated by its conformity with the event of Auschwitz. For instance, ". . . the biblical concept of a just God who is the omnipotent judge of the world and the ultimate author of human history"[6] must be rejected, because there is simply no way to harmonize it with Auschwitz. In addition, what the theologian extrapolates from this event becomes the critical tool by which he appraises current theologies and theodicies still unborn.

In this context, ethnic suffering in general and the horror of Auschwitz in particular actually serve as a normative vehicle of revelation; ethnic suffering is the indispensable mirror in which the essential structures of reality are illumined for the theologian to observe and record. The symbol of Auschwitz also determines what is theologically possible and, thereby, the general framework of the theological system as well as the materials that can be used to construct the system.

Clearly Rubenstein's method here collapses theology into theodicy; theology becomes an extended theodicy, as I believe it should be. It is clear, too, that the importance he assigns to Auschwitz indicates his adoption of the counterevidential model. For these reasons it is important to consider now what modifications he thinks are necessary for traditional biblical and Jewish theology to assimilate ethnic suffering into their respective systems:

Rubenstein's major theological reconstruction is to abandon the time-honored theology of history in the Judaeo-Christian tradition, namely God as active in and sovereign over human history. His reason for scrapping the biblical concept of history is clear. When one tries to apply its formula to Jewish suffering and to Auschwitz, he is required to support positions that are unacceptable. Its concept of God's overruling sovereignty ultimately makes God responsible for the crimes of human history. It leads in the final analysis to the conclusion that Hitler is God's redemptive agent!

> Heinrich Gruber, Dean of the Evangelical Church of East and West Berlin, . . . dramatized the consequence of accepting the normative Judaeo-Christian theology in the light of the death camps. . . . If I believed in God as the omnipotent author of the historical drama and Israel as His Chosen People, I had to accept Dean Gruber's conclusion that it was God's will that Hitler committed six million Jews to slaughter.[7]

To avoid this "theological obscenity," Rubenstein finds it theologically preferable to jettison this theology of history and replace it with one capable of accommodating the death camps. The candidate he advances effectively eliminates God's activity in human affairs; the biblical God of history is replaced by a God of nature. The unobscure purpose of his theological reconstruction is to nullify the operation of suprahuman forces that control human history. Thus his new theology of history makes man functionally ultimate as far as the historical drama is concerned:

> No more will God be seen as the transcendent lord of nature, controlling it as if it were a marionette at the end of a string. God will be seen as the source and life of nature, the being of beings which ephemerally and epiphenomenally are nature's self-expression.[8]

Rubenstein's new theological formula also eliminates the biblical concept of a God of love and mercy working for man's ultimate good, in favor of the cannibal God Earth:

> The only God I believe in is the cannibal Mother Goddess of earth who brings forth her children only to consume them and take them back unto herself.[9] We stand in a cold, silent, unfeeling cosmos, unaided by any powerful power beyond our own resources. After Auschwitz what else can a Jew say about God?[10]

And instead of a redeeming Messiah who ushers in the New Age where death and suffering are no more, Rubenstein affirms a Messiah whose act of redemption is the death of man:

> There is only one Messiah who redeems us from the travail and the limitations of human existence. Surely he will come. He is the angel of Death. Death is the true Messiah and the land of the dead the place of God's true kingdom. Only in death are we redeemed from the vicissitudes of human existence.[11]

Rubenstein's treatment of ethnic suffering raises several crucial issues for black theology. If we make the issue of ethnic suffering the point of departure for theologizing and if we endorse the counterevidential approach to theologizing, are we forced to the specific conclusions about God, man, and history that Rubenstein affirms? If we say no, then we are obliged to show that Rubenstein's analysis is not exhaustive. This is the immediate task: to question the exhaustive character of his theological reconstruction, not its truth value. If we say no, we are also obliged to give a theological formula that can in fact accommodate Auschwitz and the death camps. That is the purpose of the next chapter of this book.

The fatal defect in Rubenstein's approach is that he moves much too quickly from the fact of Jewish suffering to specific ontological and anthropological conclusions. I agree with him that ethnic suffering raises the fundamental *question* of the morality of God and the mode of His activity in human affairs, but it is not my position that we can extract the *answer* to this theological puzzle by inspecting that suffering. It is precisely at this point in the theological enterprise that the multievidentiality of suffering must be recognized and given its appropriate weight. Rubenstein's hasty movement from Auschwitz to the cannibal Mother Earth illegitimately bypasses other interpretive options, such as divine anti-Semitism; a personal God who controls history and dislikes Jews can easily account for the horror of Auschwitz. In fact, his failure to consider and refute other explanations raises a serious question about the internal consistency of his system. His approach was to make Jewish suffering the point of departure and then determine which concepts of God could be squared with it; a specific concept of God is not brought to the analysis of Jewish suffering in an a priori way. However, it is questionable if this approach is carried through consistently. There is a strong hint that Rubenstein, in point of fact, brings to his analysis the concept of God's intrinsic benevolence, and this is the reason an interpretive framework of divine anti-Semitism is never considered. Consider the following statement, which is meaningful only if God's intrinsic goodness is presupposed: "To see any purpose in the death camps is to regard the most demonic, anti-human explosion in all history as a meaningful expression of God's purpose. The idea is simply too obscene for me to accept."[12]

Secular humanism can also accommodate the major items on Rubenstein's agenda, but he rejects this position after careful consideration. It is instructive to examine the basis for his rejection.

No doubt some readers will regard this issue as of academic interest only, with no real importance for black theology. I would strongly deny that this is the case. Rubenstein rejects secular humanism because he is mistaken about its intrinsic character; in point of fact, there is little difference between his own position and those I would identify with prominent humanists such as Jean-Paul Sartre and Albert Camus. I believe, too, that the same misconceptions are held by many black religionists; hence their belief that only theism can provide a sound basis for black religion. It is therefore necessary and desirable to commence a campaign to make this position theologically respectable, and to do this means that the widely held misunderstandings that surround it must be called into question.

Rubenstein acknowledges that secular humanism provides the appropriate theology of history his position demands. Nonetheless he repudiates it, because he believes that the actualization of its principles would lead to the annihilation of Judaism. But his argument against secular humanism makes a crucial presupposition that is not warranted: He concludes that Judaism requires an irreducible particularity; it demands a climate in which ethnic differences are honored. Secular humanism, however, fosters a climate of commonality and cultural sameness, where ethnic differences would be lost.

Obviously, black theology harbors the same fears, and if Rubenstein's description is correct, secular humanism could never be an appropriate vehicle for black theology. I am confident, however, that the error lies in Rubenstein's description and does not inhere in the essential principles of humanism. To highlight Rubenstein's error, I wish to give an extended statement of his criticism and then direct the reader to some pertinent passages in Sartre, who, I submit, affirms the very position that Rubenstein himself endorses.

> We reject secular humanism, not because we have a less tragic view of ultimate human destiny, but because secular humanism is unmindful of the full determinants of the person, which root each individual irrevocably in a definite situation involving the shared vicissitudes of history, culture, and psychological perspective. Affirmation of secular humanism involves a dilution of the facticities of each man's specific human situation. The secular humanist is most cognizant of what he shares with all

men. But one must be a particular kind of man with a limited, concrete life-situation to be a man at all. The concept of humanity in general is a meaningless and tragic abstraction as Hannah Arendt has illustrated. . . . Those Jews who achieved the longed-for goal of the secular humanists . . . found that this was no messianic blessing but the final preparation for annihilation.[13]

Regarding the first point—secular humanism does not give sufficient weight to man's facticity—I would simply refer the reader to Sartre's *Being and Nothingness,* particularly to the section entitled appropriately "Freedom and Facticity: The Situation."[14] Rubenstein's charge cannot stand in the face of the argument presented there. Indeed, when this section of Sartre's work is read, one will quickly see that his position and Rubenstein's are identical with respect to the category of human facticity.

But Rubenstein's major concern is the anti-Semitic and genocidal potential of secular humanism, and it is this alleged potential that troubles the black theologian as well. To counter this objection, it is necessary only to cite the following passage from Sartre's *Anti-Semite and Jew,* which coincides exactly with Rubenstein's own position:

The Jews have one friend, however, the democrat. But he is a feeble protector. No doubt he proclaims that all men have equal rights, . . . but his own declarations show the weakness of his position. . . . He recognizes neither Jew, nor Arab, nor Negro, . . . but only man— man always the same in all times and all places. . . . The democrat . . . fails to see the particular case. . . . It follows that his defense of the Jew saves the latter as man and annihilates him as Jew. . . . This means that he wants to separate the Jew from his religion, from his family, from his ethnic community. . . . For a Jew, conscious and proud of being Jewish, asserting a claim to be a member of the Jewish community without ignoring on that account the bonds which unite him to the

national community, there may not be so much difference between the anti-Semite and the democrat. The
former wishes to destroy him as a man and leave nothing
in him but the Jew. . . ; the latter wishes to destroy
him as a Jew and leave nothing in him but the man.
. . . Thus there may be detected in the most liberal
democrat a tinge of anti-Semitism; he is hostile to the
Jew to the extent that the latter thinks of himself as a
Jew.[15]

A similar argument could be presented to show the fundamental similarity between Rubenstein's position and Camus's,
but this would fall outside the scope of my concern, which is
only to indicate that Rubenstein's theological framework is
not exhaustive.

I must confess a special concern to demonstrate that Rubenstein's analysis is not the only model that can accommodate
ethnic suffering, because I see in his viewpoint real dangers
for a theology of liberation. His position appears to lead to a
deterministic pessimism—he would say, no doubt, realism—
with quietism as its logical outcome:

We are born but to perish. . . . I do not understand
Altizer's optimism. The Kingdom lies ahead of us, but it
is not the new reality he supposes. It is the nothingness
out of which we have come and to which we are in-
escapably destined to return. . . . This world will forever remain a place of pain, suffering, alienation, and
ultimate defeat. . . . This is the only world we will ever
know.[16]

This account of the ruthless inevitability and depressing
perpetuity of suffering and pain hardly provides a motive
for the corrective efforts inherent in a theology of liberation.
Rather, one is motivated more to defeatism and to quietism.
While I must acknowledge that Rubenstein's own formula
for Jewish liberation does not endorse quietism, I do question
the consistency of his sociopolitical pronouncements and their

ontological foundation. It also appears that he has substituted one form of determinism for another. He castigates the determinism implicit in the traditional biblical concept of God as the ultimate author of human history, and the optimism it entails. Yet I find it difficult to differentiate between the determinism of the God of nature he accepts and that of the God of history he rejects.

XII

HUMANOCENTRIC THEISM:
A THEISTIC FRAMEWORK FOR ETHNIC
SUFFERING

John Hick suggests that the function of a theodicy is primarily apologetic; its purpose is not to create faith, but "to preserve an existing faith"[1] and keep it from being overcome by contrary facts of human experience. This also appears to be a primary concern of the current black theologians: to show that belief in Christian theism is not fatally undermined by the fact of ethnic suffering. They recognize, however, that a black theology must concern itself with an additional demand, a purpose that Hick does not even consider, namely the liberation of the oppressed.

The previous chapters have questioned the adequacy of their respective systems to meet both the needs of apologetics and also the requirements of liberation. Thus the concern in this chapter is to present a more reliable and consistent theological framework to fulfill these needs; this will be done under the rubric of humanocentric theism.

Several qualifications, however, must be given at the outset: It must be clearly understood that I am presenting a suggested theistic framework and not my own humanistic model, though I regard the two to be similar. Further, I see the task of theodicy in a somewhat different light from Hick. For me, the emphasis is not primarily apologetic, but ontological validation. I see the need to present the most accurate explanation of ethnic suffering, but not to prop up a sagging belief system, parts of which ought to be allowed to wither away because of their inadequacies as sound accounts of crucial human realities. For the present moment, however, I aim at a theological construction for the theists in contemporary black religion.

Finally, I acknowledge that humanocentric theism does not honor every pressing demand of a contemporary black theodicy. Nor, for that matter, does my own humanist position. I advance the position of humanocentric theism and secular humanism as more trustworthy than the theological models that inform the extant black theologies. Moreover, the several inconsistencies we noted in the latter seem to be absent from humanocentric theism. Its special merits are its capacity to eliminate the charge of divine racism and its unambiguous impulse against quietism. It thus becomes necessary to describe the essentials of this hybrid of humanism and theism, illuminate its value for a black theodicy, and appraise the available black theologies from its perspective.

The Essentials of Humanocentric Theism

The most fruitful way to begin this description is to identify the essential tenets of humanocentric theism and illustrate each with representative statements from selected theologians. I apologize in advance for the extensive quotations. These are necessary, however, because I am attempting to define a new variety of theism. I am also assigning a theological label to thinkers that they may not acknowledge. In this situation it seems desirable to let their own words speak for themselves and thus allow each reader to decide if I have accurately extracted their viewpoint and formulated an appropriate terminology for their position.

As the qualifier suggests, the distinctive feature of humano-

centric theism is the exalted status it assigns to man and his
activity. Its specific tenets are simply different ways of identifying the prominence of man in crucial areas. It will become
clear that this variety of theism transfers to man areas of
control and some of the primary functions that previous theological traditions reserved for God alone. Here, we will see,
is an explicit affirmation of the functional ultimacy of man.[2]
The opposite theological position could best be described as
theocentric theism, not humanism. Theocentric theism would
argue for God's controlling and overruling sovereignty over
the essential aspects of the human situation, especially human
destiny. The essential difference between these rival forms of
theism is how each defines the role, status, and value of
human freedom relative to divine freedom.

Humanocentric theism does assign an exalted status to man,
particularly to human freedom, but this status—and here we
come to its theistic ground—is the consequence of God's will,
and it conforms to His ultimate purpose and plan for mankind.
A passage from Martin Buber, the Jewish existentialist, accents
this feature of humanocentric theism:

> Man can choose God and he can reject God. . . . That
> man has the power to lead the world to perdition implies
> that he has power to lead the world to redemption. . . .
> These two powers of man constitute the actual admission
> of man into mightiness. . . . The fact remains that the
> creation of this being, man, means that God has made
> room for a *codetermining power,* for a starting-point for
> events. . . . Does that mean that God cannot redeem
> the world without man's help? It means that God *wills* not
> that He could do that. Has God need of man for His work?
> He wills to have need of man. . . . Does this mean that
> God has given away one particle of His power to deter-
> mine the course of events? We only ask that question
> when we are busy subsuming God under our logical cate-
> gories. In the moment when He breaks through we have
> an immediate experience of our freedom, and yet in these

moments we also know by an immediate experience that God's hand has carried us.[3]

Several features of this passage enable us to begin a progressive development of the essential tenets of humanocentric theism. We note first the point already cited, the exalted status assigned to man and his efforts relative to the fulfillment of God's plan. Man is a codetermining power, and he possesses this ontological status by virtue of his creation. That is to say, we are describing the common situation of man, not the specialized situation of salvation or eschatological consummation, which is reserved for the elect. This is another way of saying that being a codetermining power is intrinsic to man's being; it is an aspect of his nature.

We will misunderstand Buber's thought, however, if we fail to accentuate his conclusion that man's codetermining status is in total conformity with the sovereignty, purpose, and will of God. Unlike the attitude of God as expressed in the Tower of Babel, God is not jealous about man reaching His level of mightiness. Giving man coresponsibility and codetermining equality in specific areas of human life need not be construed as a theological assault against the traditional attributes of God, in particular His sovereignty or omnipotence. Indeed we will see that certain interpreters of Christian faith argue that God's endowment of man as a codetermining center of power is the most authentic expression of his sovereignty.

In this connection, it is helpful to consider how Buber specifies the power of man relative to God; man appears to function in an essential way relative to his own redemption:

> We are dependent on grace, but we do not do God's will when we take it upon ourselves to begin with grace instead of beginning with ourselves. Only our beginning, our having begun, poor as it is, leads us to grace. . . . The impulse to redemption must proceed from below.[4]

Buber, however, seemingly wants to restrict man's activity to the "starting-point" of redemption, whereas representatives to be considered subsequently want to push the powers of man beyond the boundaries Buber wants to maintain.

Buber's analysis spotlights another tenet of humanocentric theism, which is also to say, a further implication of the functional ultimacy of man. Note the emphasis placed upon the *activity* and *choice* of man. They are necessary conditions, not for peripheral human concerns but for man's highest good itself.

I also find the position of humanocentric theism to be central to the thought of Harvey Cox as expressed in *The Secular City*. An examination of his position adds another dimension to this theological hybrid. Like Buber, Cox accents man's status as a codetermining power, but he grounds this status in the covenant relation rather than the doctrine of creation. Drawing particularly upon some incarnational motifs, Cox also attaches distinctly Christian themes to the position of humanocentric theism. It is important to emphasize this fact, since some might erroneously conclude that a Christological emphasis is fatal to this form of theism.

Recent discussions of the concept of the covenant in the Old Testament suggest . . . that Yahweh was willing to stoop so low as to work in tandem with man, to work on a team, no matter how poorly the human partner was working out. It can certainly be said that in Jesus of Nazareth God did show that he was willing to take man's side of the unfilled covenant, to become the junior partner in the asymmetrical relationship. He who is "high and lifted up" suggests that . . . he is willing to put himself in the position of working within a group, . . . of needing someone to carry his cross. . . . The idea of an I-You relationship between God and man is strongly hinted by the language of Galatians 4. . . . In this passage man is viewed as a son and heir. The emphasis is on *son* as opposed to child, and on *heir* as having assumed responsibility. This implies that the strict vertical relationship which informs a father's relationship to his minor

boy is discarded for the adult relationship which obtains
between a grown man and his father. . . . Man's relationship derives from the work they do together.[5]

It is clear that Cox gives man an exalted status in the divine
design. To be accurate, man appears to enjoy more clout in
Cox's scheme than in Buber's. Whereas Buber emphasizes
man's codetermination in terms of his necessity to begin, Cox's
metaphor of the partnership and heir is more suggestive of
man's codeterminative responsibility throughout. Indeed the
metaphor can also be pushed to mean that the father, God,
has bequeathed the family business to his heirs, and thus we
are faced with these questions: Do the heirs, man, simply hold
the business in trust, with God determining the conditions of
the trust? Or has God fully released his sovereign reins over the
business, leaving its affairs totally to his children, which
is to say, in human hands? Cox is not clear on this point. Other
passages suggest the view that man is the ultimate determiner
of human history. At least this is a possible inference from
his claim that "in Jesus, God is teaching man to get along without Him, to become mature, freed from infantile dependencies,
fully human."[6] By becoming a man in Jesus of Nazareth, God
affirms that his activity in human history from then on is played
out in the activities of particular men. Man, then, is functionally ultimate relative to human history.

A similar conclusion can be drawn from Cox's concepts of
"the disenchantment of nature," "the Exodus as the desacralization of politics," and "the Sinai Covenant as the deconsecration
of values." Essential to each of these biblical developments is
the extension of the functional ultimacy of man over an area
that had previously been wholly under the sway of the divine.
The disenchantment of nature establishes that nature is "available for man's use" and that man is its "master and com-
mander."[7] The desacralization of politics delivers political
affairs from divine hands, as once thought, and into human
hands. We move, as it were, from the politics of God to the
politics of man. And the consequence of the deconsecration

of values is to "place the responsibility for the forging of human values, like the forging of political systems, in man's own hands."[8] Thus the functional ultimacy of man relative to values and history is affirmed.

This enlargement of human power and responsibility leads to a probing question that Cox raises himself and that the advocate of humanocentric theism must also address: Is God simply another way of talking about man? Are divine acts reducible in sum to human acts? Cox's answer insists upon God's independence over against man. This is heightened even more in that man's status as codeterminer, as in Buber, is given to him. "The freedom of man depends upon the prior freedom of God."[9] Further, "God is not man, and man can only really be *'responseable'* . . . *before* someone. Man, in order to be free and responsible, which means to be man, must answer to that which is not man."[10] But this avoids the crucial issue that must be addressed to determine the exact parameters of the position of humanocentric theism, and that is, in what sense, if any, does God retain a veto power over man?[11]

Howard Burkle is willing to affirm explicitly what is only hinted in Cox's analysis. In a real sense, according to Burkle, God's sovereignty is limited by the choices and acts of man. God, in his system, "would have to be uncertain about a number of the details of the future, willing to improvise and accommodate his will to the contingencies of the world, and in some respects unable to accomplish his will at all." Moreover, this type of God "cannot guarantee the ultimate triumph of good. If man—and whatever free creatures there may be in the universe—are able to oppose God, then the good may remain forever blocked."[12]

But this limitation of God's sovereignty is self-imposed. It is the consequence of God's decision and will to respect the freedom He gave to man. This means that He relates Himself to man in terms of persuasion and not coercion. A persuading God seeks "to arouse and sustain and co-ordinate the self-actualization activities" of man. And self-actualization for

Burkle means for more than God's presenting Himself as an object of choice:

> In the relation of persuasion, we give the other person some distance, we let him be over against us. We allow and encourage him to exercise and perfect his powers of self-determination. . . . In a word, we treat him as a co-creator with ourselves. Of course this obtains only where the future can be left open. . . . God communicates, solicits, and tries by rational means to affect our choices. We are always responding to influences which are encouraging us to think, weigh and choose. Whenever a man seizes the possibilities of freedom and acts from within his own being, he is certifying the persuasive activity of God.[13]

Burkle is not afraid to draw the obvious consequence of divine persuasion rather than the apparently contrary divine attribute of sovereignty, which is the elimination of God's overruling omnipotence. Human destiny is not already determined by God's purpose. God's blueprint—if He has one—will be actualized only if He can persuade man, in a non-coercive way, to choose what God thinks is best for man.

Yet Burkle, like Cox and Buber, detects no disharmony between this expanded concept of human freedom and divine sovereignty, for, as indicated, this limitation is self-imposed. What is advanced here is a redefinition of the traditional concept of omnipotence to fit the requirements of the freedom of God *and* man; this constitutes another essential feature of humanocentric theism.

> Persuasion seems a kind of impotence. This objection is based on a misconception of power. . . . Among persons, persuasion and not compulsion is the highest form of power. Compulsion is a last resort. . . . Persuasion—the art of influencing another toward the better without deceit, threat or bribery—is power indeed.[14]

Kierkegaard long before made the point better by insisting

that the independence Burkle wishes to reserve for man is demanded by the divine benevolence. "Omnipotence," he says, "alone can take itself back while giving, and this relationship is nothing but the independence of the recipient. God's omnipotence is therefore his goodness. For goodness means to give absolutely, yet in such a way that by taking oneself back one makes the recipient independent."[15]

Burkle's concept of divine sovereignty becomes clearer if we recognize that he differentiates between the exercise of God's omnipotence at the level of ontology, i.e. efficient causality, and its operation at the level of human history. This description is also evidence for the earlier claim that humanocentric theism does not make God simply a projection of human reality. Ontologically speaking, man is and remains the subordinate creature in so far as his existence comes from a transcendent source:[16]

> God is the efficient cause of the world in that he is the agent, mover or source by which the world receives its being. There is no question of persuasion here; forbearance would mean non-existence for the world. . . . Efficient causality, as the activity which grounds all being, must therefore be a sovereign or originating act. . . . Efficient causality . . . is the first step which the Persuader must take in order to have before Him someone to persuade. . . . Even though the creature exists whether or not he wishes to, . . . suicide is always possible. Also nihilism and other attitudes which deny the importance and reality of existence are possible. The creature retains a veto even though he had nothing to do with the determination that gave him being.[17]

Several features of humanocentric theism have been considered: its affirmation of a delegated ontological status to man as cocreator of essential features of human existence; its emphasis upon the activity, choice, and freedom of man; and the reinterpretation of the concept of divine sovereignty and omnipotence. One final item must be discussed, and that is the similarity of humanocentric theism and secular humanism. It has already been indicated that both positions affirm the principle of the functional ultimacy of man in human history and/ or the arena of values. Burkle accents this similarity when he acknowledges that there is no significant difference between his variety of theism, on the one hand, and atheism or humanism on the other:

> The effects which we have attributed to the Persuader might just as well . . . arise from indeterminacy. Men will have independence, distance, and the opportunity to choose for themselves—all the elements of an environment conducive to self-determined activity—if there is no God at all. . . . Pragmatically speaking, believing in a persuading God and believing in no God at all come to very much the same thing.[18]

Cox makes a similar admission when he allows that the essential features of the biblical concept of secularization, e.g. the deconsecration of values, can develop from either a theistic or a non-theistic perspective. "Marxist theism, despite fundamental differences from Christianity, performs an analogous cultural function by disenchanting nature, while its theory of politics also desacralizes ruling regimes. The same is true in the deconsecration of values."[19]

Theodicy and Humanocentric Theism

Having described some of the essential components of humanocentric theism, it is now possible to indicate its value as a framework for a black theodicy. First and foremost, (1) it provides a *consistent* framework for accommodating the freedom of man, an indispensable ingredient of a theology of liberation. The current black theologians recognize that their systems must absorb the freedom of man as a central tenet, but they fail to accomplish this in a manner that is logically compatible with the remainder of their respective systems. This inherent ambiguity, I submit, will surface as soon as they relate their pronouncements on divine sovereignty to their assertions about human freedom.

(2) Whereas the theodicies of the present black theologians do not successfully handle the issue of divine racism, humanocentric theism provides a sturdy refutation. It accomplishes this by removing God's overruling sovereignty from human history. The concept of divine persuasion and the functional ultimacy of man leads to a theory of human history in which the interplay of human power centers and alignments is decisive. In this context, racism is traced, causally, to human forces. Divine responsibility for the crimes of human history is thus eliminated. In fact, this appears to be the only way to avoid the proposition that Cone finds fatal for a black theodicy, which is the acceptance of any view that even indirectly places divine approval on the sufferings of man, particularly black man.

There is a decided plus for making racism the consequence of human activities alone. Any analysis of racism that fails to recognize it as the consequence of a gross imbalance of power is unacceptable. Racism, like all oppression, is an exercise in power in which one group can pursue its priorities unchecked by a coequal force.

(3) Humanocentric theism also cuts off a theological and moral escape often used by the white oppressor. He can no longer point to anything but men as the sustaining force behind racism. In like manner, unless blacks see themselves as coresponsible for their plight in so far as they do not lynch the lyncher, unless they recognize the power resident in themselves as human centers of freedom and in their communities as potential collective sources of transforming power, blacks will not take the necessary steps to free themselves from the chains of racism and oppression. This "all is in man's hands" philosophy admittedly has a certain potential for defeatism, but it is also an effective, perhaps necessary, remedy for quietism.

Humanocentric theism provides the most effective antibiotic to the virus of quietism. Several conditions were cited earlier that underlie the impulse to quietism: when one regards his suffering as positive relative to his salvation; when one is uncertain about the positive or negative quality of the suffering from God's perspective, when it is believed that someone else is effecting one's highest good, and when it is thought that it is impossible to terminate one's suffering. In the context of humanocentric theism, the first two conditions vanish, because it is man who now makes the decisive judgment about the quality of suffering. This is not to say that all doubt is removed; humanocentric theism is not an absolute guarantee against the slings of relativism and skepticism. However, it does appear to be the case that it is decidedly easier to validate the character of suffering vis-à-vis other men than vis-à-vis the divine.

The third factor, human activity is not necessary, also evaporates in view of the conclusion that God's activity in human history is restricted to persuasion. Human activity is thus decisive for one's salvation or liberation.

The final feature, human activity is impotent, is also countered effectively by humanocentric theism, though other black theologians may well conclude that it runs against the psychological needs of oppressed blacks. Quietism, based on man's inevitable failure, presupposes that the structures of reality exclude success. Recall for a moment the figure of Sisyphus, whose efforts were constantly frustrated by the ultimate structures of reality.

The consequence of humanocentric theism is to remove God from anyone's side. History becomes open-ended and multivalued, capable of supporting either oppression or liberation, racism or brotherhood. The available black theologies, however, have advanced a different view, insisting that an oppressed group requires the belief that ultimate reality is on its side in its struggle for liberation. Given the fact that blacks in America are a powerless numerical minority, the support of ultimate reality seems to be an absolute necessity. A David is reluctant to challenge Goliath unless he believes that God will tip the scales in his favor.

In this sense, some will argue that humanocentric theism reintroduces the specter of quietism, for its view of divine neutrality undermines the motivation of blacks to move against the powerful white majority; humanocentric theism leads to defeatism, and the latter to quietism. I would respond that the claim of God's support for black liberation lacks substance until the black theologians refute the charge of divine racism. Their failure to provide a convincing rebuttal, along with their question-begging argument for divine sanction of black freedom, eliminates any real ground for black hope. Until they provide a more effective theodicy, the choice is between (a) a black hope based on God as a white racist and (b) one based on God as functionally neutral relative to human affairs. If these are the alternatives, then the choice open to us seems clear-cut.

(4) Not to be overlooked is the potential of humanocentric theism as a response to the emergent secularism of our time. Black theologians have not yet responded to this issue. Some argue that they need not, others that they should not. However, I see secularism as an entry that will become more formidable in black religion, and the present black theologies are ill equipped to handle it.

The Theodicy of John Hick

Some readers, no doubt, will ask why we have jumped from the defective theodicies of the black theologians to the position of humanocentric theism without considering other possibilities, such as the theology of hope of Jürgen Moltmann or John Hick's statement of "A Theodicy for Today." In response, I would say that the discussion of options other than those proposed by the black theologians falls outside the scope of my task. The research for this study, however, surveyed what I take to be the total spectrum of theodicies in the West. I must confess that I do not find the proposal of Hick and the theologians of hope to be serviceable for a black theology.

The classical theodicies are deficient because they primarily treat the issue of human suffering in general; the issue of ethnic suffering is not investigated. When a theodicy is transferred from the arena of general human suffering to ethnic suffering, its utility vanishes.

Though the black theologians speak of a theology of hope and make use of some insights from this school of theology, it is asserted that the theologians of hope do not provide the appropriate model for oppressed blacks. J. Deotis Roberts, for instance, records Moltmann's admission that his theology emerges from a different cultural context. With this understanding, Roberts concludes that "the so-called theology of hope has a good psychological ring for a hopeless people, but it does not, however, ring true to the black experience. Like many other 'transport' theological movements, it belongs to another situation."[20]

Special attention must be afforded Hick's proposal for theodicy, since it is written with the broad spectrum of classical theodicies in the background. Its flaws, however, are fatal as far as a black theodicy is concerned: First, Hick does not relate his statement of theodicy to the demands of a theology of liberation. If this had been central to his purpose, I question if his position would be the same. Indeed the same claim can be registered with reference to the total class of traditional theodicies. A cursory examination of the outline of his theodicy will reveal its other shortcomings: Hick interprets human suffering as a form of spiritual pedagogy. Man, in his view, is spiritually immature and requires a period of development to become the being God intended in creation. Thus the world, with its suffering, is the "divinely created sphere of soul-making . . . a vale of soul-making."[21]

But collapsing suffering into a form of spiritual pedagogy misses the impact of the maldistribution of ethnic suffering. Is this to suggest that those who suffer most in this world are somehow slower learners? Yet a more serious flaw is Hick's eschatological emphasis and its question-begging approach to the benevolence of God. He simply dismisses the issue raised by Auschwitz, arguing that it was in no sense willed by God:

These events were utterly evil, wicked, devilish . . . and

unforgiveable. . . . It would have been better . . . if they had never happened. Most certainly God did not want those who committed these fearful crimes against humanity to act as they did. His purpose for the world was retarded by them and the power of evil within it increased. Undoubtly He saw with anger and grief the sufferings so wilfully inflicted upon the people of His ancient choice. . . .[22]

We can know, however, that God is benevolent and is horrified by Auschwitz only eschatologically. Suffering, for Hick, is evil or good depending upon whether it furthers or hinders God's plan for creation. But the nature of that plan and the relation of earthly sufferings to it is cloaked in mystery until after death. "We have to say simply that the incomprehensible mingling in human experience of good and evil, pain and pleasure . . . continues in all its characteristic and baffling ambiguity throughout life and ends only with death."[23] But, again, we cannot legitimately affirm that the plan for creation is good and that God does not in fact will Auschwitz or black suffering, until the eschaton.

It is also interesting to note how Hick treats the problem of the maldistribution of suffering. An eschatological illumination will inform those who suffer disproportionately that their excessive suffering is justified in the light of an infinite good that justifies "any finite suffering":

What is being suggested here . . . is that these sufferings —which for some people are immense and for others relatively slight—will in the end lead to the enjoyment of a common good which will be unending and therefore unlimited and which will be seen by its participants as justifying all that has been endured on the way to it. The good eschaton will not be a reward or compensation proportioned to each individual's trials, but an infinite good that would render worthwhile any finite suffering endured in the course of attaining it.[23]

Is this not the "pie in the sky" theodicy in a new form?

Nor should the reader overlook the theological balm Hick offers to the victims of Auschwitz, namely "the assurance that God's good purpose . . . has not been defeated" by Hitler's efforts and that the victims are "alive in the realms beyond our world . . . and will have their place in the final fulfillment of God's creation."[24]

Need I go on?

Black Theology, Humanocentric Theism, and Theological Reconstruction

The concern in this final section is to analyze briefly the consequences of humanocentric theism for the available black theologies. In particular, I wish to identify the theological reconstruction that would follow the acceptance of this form of theism.

At the outset, it is significant to note that some of the essential components of humanocentric theism are already present in most of the black theologies. Only Washington's emphatic description of God's overruling sovereignty seems to oppose it at all points, though his theological development after *The Politics of God* may belie this conclusion. Cone, however, seems to opt for the precise concept of omnipotence that informs humanocentric theism, and it is noteworthy that the following citation is the concluding paragraph of the section where he discusses divine providence and theodicy: "Omnipotence," he argues, "does not refer to God's absolute power to accomplish what he wants. But as John Macquarrie says, omnipotence is 'the power to let something stand out from nothing and to be.' "[25] And if Major Jones's concept of a helpless God is understood in the context of its source (which is Bonhoeffer's emphasis upon the powerlessness and suffering of God), a central aspect of his system also coincides with humanocentric theism. Roberts, too, speaks of man as "co-creator with God" and sees this status as the theological correlate of the goodness of creation.

These elements of humanocentric theism, however, can eas-

ily be matched by theological claims that assert something akin
to theocentric theism. Major Jones, for instance, argues for a
God who is strong enough to determine the outcome of the
future both within and beyond history."[26] Perhaps the category
that harmonizes these apparently contradictory poles of his
thought is the ultimate potency of suffering love. And though
Cone exhorts blacks to liberate themselves by any means necessary, there also stands this statement: "We do not read far in
the biblical tradition without recognizing that the God-man relationship is to be understood exclusively in terms of what God
does for man and not what man does for himself or for God."[27]
Elsewhere he speaks of the "certainty" that God is on the side
of oppressed blacks, thus insuring their liberation. It is hoped
that the black theologians will address themselves again to the
issue of the relation of human and divine freedom and remove
the ambiguity that envelops this segment of their thought.

We can also identify the primary concepts the black theologians must abandon if humanocentric theism is accepted. The
concept of God as for the oppressed must be relinquished if
this means that the oppressed are the unique object of God's
activity in a manner that differs from persuasion. This may
seem like a lot to give up, but consider the other alternative:
If the black theologians emphasize the theocentric side of their
thought, if God's overruling sovereignty is affirmed, then they
are forced to account for the maldistribution of black suffering
in the face of His coercive sovereignty. They must answer these
questions: Why has God not eliminated black suffering? Why
are the oppressed always with us?

Talk about the inevitable liberation of blacks must also be
muted. The actual character of human history is the product
of human choices and actions. Human progress or moral improvement is not assured, particularly where black prospects
are at stake. Black hope may run afoul of the changing and
adapting forms of racism in the future.

The black theologian also will not have the luxury, as now
appears to be the case, of selecting specific historical events
and identifying them as God's handiwork, while dismissing

those which refute his argument as the actions of sinful men.

No doubt two arguments will be directed against this suggested theological model, arguments that testify for me that the black theologians are torn by conflicting theological agendas. What is being done, some will say, is to remove all hope from black religion. But it must also be considered that to speak of God as the ground for black hope—without the prior refutation of divine racism—is sheer theological illusion and pipe dreaming. Have we removed a substantial hope, or exposed a comfortable but ill-advised illusion?

That humanocentric theism does not harmonize with the present belief system of the black church will also be argued. I do not find this a formidable challenge. The crucial issue is not the continuity of a proposed theological position with the faith of the present generation of black churchmen, but its humanizing and liberating quality. I trust that it is now possible to say in the light of our study that perhaps some of the cherished beliefs of black people are in fact part and parcel of their oppression!

I would also note that the black theologians examined here also advance concepts that they acknowledge might not sit well with their black readers in the church. Consider, for example, Cone's claim that some black people will find the core of his system "hard to handle," namely that God is identified with their struggle for freedom."[28] And this is so because they still are tied to the beliefs of the oppressor. Obviously, the same argument could be utilized by the advocate of humanocentric theism. Similarly Major Jones admits that the concept of the suffering and helpless God, a central motif in his system, is "to ask for a different kind of faith than that which is traditionally characterized in the black church."[29] In sum, does humanocentric theism depart radically from aspects of the black theologians' own position?

EPILOGUE

There is probably an unavoidable hint of arrogance in anyone who proposes his work as a prolegomenon. But any arrogance that might motivate this study is tempered by a number of factors: first and foremost is the recognition of the fate of previous prolegomena; they have become grist for the mill of subsequent prolegomena.

My real purpose is not to preclude further debate by providing *the truth*, but to suggest an interpretive forum in which that debate can occur. It is also the case that in a new discipline, such as black theology, any criticism of the present systems, of necessity, assumes the character of a prolegomenon. Accordingly a critic must accept this unintentional role with its suspicion of arrogance—or else remain silent. For reasons that I trust are now clear, I have chosen not to be silent.

On with the debate!

Note to Prologue

1. W. E. B. Du Bois, "Litany at Atlanta," in *Darkwater; Voices from Within the Veil* (New York: Harcourt, Brace and Howe, 1920), pp. 25 ff.

Notes to Introduction

1. Theodicy, from the Greek *theos,* God, and *dikē,* justice, is the common term for the field of inquiry that deals with the issue of evil and human suffering. Most often it signifies the attempt to account for human suffering and evil in the framework of one's affirmations about the nature and activity of God. I shall use the term, however, in a different sense. My stipulative definition is given on pp. xviii–xx of this book.

2. For a discussion of black humanists see pp. 29–44 of this book.

3. James H. Cone, *The Spirituals and the Blues* (New York: Seabury Press, 1972), p. 109.

4. Bertrand Russell's essay "A Free Man's Worship" helped, for instance, to clarify the concept of a demonic deity. See p. 66 of this book.

5. Richard Rubenstein, *After Auschwitz* (New York: Bobbs-Merrill Company, 1966).

6. The point is not essential for my argument, but I would regard black suffering as more severe than Jewish suffering. Basil Davidson, for instance, estimates that slavery before and after embarkation cost fifty million black souls. *Black Mother* (Boston: Little, Brown & Company, 1961), p. 80. Yet numbers alone do not tell the total story. I do not detect decimation of Jewish culture and tradition, but decimation of black culture and tradition characterizes life in America.

7. Frederick Sontag, *God, Why Did You Do That?* (Philadelphia: Westminster Press, 1970).

8. Frederick Sontag, *The God of Evil* (New York: Harper & Row, 1970).

9. Cited in *New Theology No. 5,* ed. by Martin E. Marty and Dean G. Peerman (New York: The Macmillan Co., 1968), p. 135.

10. It is well to recall here the perceptive observation of John Bowker. "If the different religions have a common factor in their treatment of suffering, it is that they start with the facts of suffering as they are, not with suffering conceived as a theoretical problem. Suffering becomes a problem when it is related to other facts or other propositions which seem to be contradicted by it." *Problems of Suffering in Religions of the World* (London: Cambridge University Press, 1970), p. 5.

11. Jürgen Moltmann, *Religion, Revolution, and the Future* (New York: Charles Scribner's Sons, 1969), p. 205.

12. John Hick, *Evil and the God of Love* (London: Macmillan & Co., 1966).

Notes to Chapter I

1. I. A. Newby, *Jim Crow's Defense: Anti-Negro Thought in America, 1900–1930* (Baton Rouge: Louisiana State University Press, 1965), p. 89.

2. Thomas F. Gossett, *Race: The History of an Idea in America* (Dallas: Southern Methodist University Press, 1963), pp. 3–4.

3. Lloyd Warner, *American Life: Dream and Reality* (Chicago: University of Chicago Press, 1953), p. 17.

4. Gossett, p. 89.

5. Cited in Gossett, p. 96.

6. I will criticize the black theologians subsequently for giving insufficient attention to the interpretation of deserved punishment or eliminating it by question-begging devices, especially when their own theological frameworks demand that the explanation of merited punishment must be taken into account.

7. Consider his *Agape and Eros* (Philadelphia: Westminster Press, 1953).

8. Albert Camus, *The Rebel,* trans. by Anthony Bower (New York: Alfred A. Knopf, 1956), pp. 32–34.

9. Samuel F. Yette, *The Choice: The Issue of Black Survival in America* (New York: Berkley Publishing Corp., 1972), p. 23.

10. This point will be explored in greater detail in the subsequent analysis of the biblical treatment of suffering, pp. 17–20 of this book.

11. Isaiah 11: 6.

12. Luke 7: 22.

13. Bernhard Anderson, *Understanding the Old Testament* (Englewood Cliffs, N.J.: Prentice-Hall, 1959), pp. 5–15.

14. John Mbiti, *New Testament Eschatology in an African Background* (London: Oxford University Press, 1971), p. 24. Emphasis supplied.

15. Proverbs 3: 12.

16. I Peter 4: 12–13.

17. I Peter 4: 1.

18. Cf. Job 14: 1–2.

19. Isaiah 53: 12.

20. Jeremiah 15: 18.

21. Mark 15: 34.

22. In this connection see the concept of catastrophic suffering, pp. 24–25 of this book.

23. Isaiah 52: 13–15.

24. Bowker, p. 11.

25. Rubenstein, p. 46.

Notes to Chapter II

1. *Negro's God.* Preface not numbered.

2. *Negro's God*, p. 218.

3. Countee Cullen, *Color* (New York: Harper & Brothers, 1925), pp. 39–40.

4. *Color*, p. 3.

5. *Color*, pp. 20–21.

6. Countee Cullen, *The Black Christ* (New York: Harper & Brothers, 1929), p. 69.

7. *Black Christ*, p. 77.

8. *Black Christ*, p. 84.

9. *Black Christ*, p. 77.

10. *Black Christ*, p. 105.

11. *Black Christ*, pp. 85–86.

12. *Black Christ*, p. 83.

13. *Black Christ*, p. 84.

14. *Black Christ*, p. 84.

15. *Black Christ*, p. 78.

16. *Black Christ*, p. 109.

17. *Black Christ*, p. 107.

18. Quoted in Carter Woodson, *Negro Orators and Their Orations* (Washington, D.C.: Associated Publishers, 1925), p. 69.

19. Nathaniel Paul, "An Address on the Celebration of the Abolition of Slavery in New York," July 5, 1827, pp. 15–16. See Library of Congress.

20. *Negro Orators,* p. 65.

21. We must not overlook the fact, however, that Paul's expectation of the liberation of blacks in the future, his eschatological expectation, is based on a concrete event of black liberation—the abolition of slavery in New York.

22. Daniel A. Payne, *Recollection of Seventy Years* (Nashville: Publishing House of the A. M. E. Sunday School Union, 1888), p. 27.

23. James Baldwin, *The Fire Next Time* (New York: The Dial Press, 1963), pp. 44–45.

24. Carter Woodson, *The Rural Negro* (Washington, D.C.: The Association for the Study of Negro Life, 1930), p. 149.

25. Nella Larsen, *Quicksand* (New York: Alfred A. Knopf, 1928), pp. 118–19.

26. See Russell's "A Free Man's Worship."

Notes to Chapter III

1. *Negro's God,* p. 155.

2. *Negro's God,* pp. 23–24.

3. *Negro's God,* p. 25. It is worth noting that Mays makes these claims in spite of the fact that he denounces the stereotyped view of black religion as an opiate and otherworldly.

4. The connection between the world view of the oppressed and their oppression is affirmed by the following: the black theologians in our study and Third World spokesmen such as Rubem Alves, *A Theology of Human Hope* (Washington: Corpus Books, 1969), and Paulo Freire, *Pedagogy of the Oppressed* (New York: Herder & Herder, 1970). One could also cite Frantz Fanon, Harvey Cox, and Richard Rubenstein.

5. See pp. 76–78 of this book.

6. William Jones, "Reconciliation and Liberation in Black Theology: Some Implications for Religious Education," *Religious Education,* 67 (September–October 1972), p. 387. The analysis of quietism here draws upon this article.

7. The discussion of humanocentric theism in Part III will amplify this point.

8. Albert Camus, *The Plague,* trans. Stuart Gilbert (New York: Alfred A. Knopf, 1958), p. 87.

9. Olive Schreiner, *The New Mother.*

10. *Plague,* p. 201.

11. *Plague,* pp. 201–2.

12. John Hick, *Evil and the God of Love* (London: Macmillan & Co., 1966), p. 371.

13. *Plague,* pp. 205–6.

14. To avoid this conclusion, it appears that the Christian must formulate a theodicy that is neither demonstrative nor a theodicy of last resort. My own resolution will emphasize the principle of the functional ultimacy of man as valuator and/or historical agent. This approach emphasizes the multievidential quality of faith principles instead of the "absolute paradox" that I find central to Kierkegaard.

15. *Plague,* p. 203.

16. Consider Bertrand Russell's description, in "A Free Man's Worship," in which the human and divine perspectives are opposed:

To Dr. Faustus in his study, Mephistophilis told the history of the Creation, saying, "The endless praises of the choirs of angels had begun to grow wearisome; for after all, did he not deserve their praise? . . . Would it not be more amusing to obtain undeserved praise, to be worshiped by beings whom he tortured? He smiled inwardly, and resolved that the great drama should be performed.

". . . Man was born, with the power of thought, the knowledge of good and evil, and the cruel thirst for worship. And Man saw that all is passing in this mad, monstrous world. . . . And Man said, 'There is a hidden purpose, could we but fathom it, and the purpose is good; for we must reverence something, and in the visible world there is nothing worthy of reverence.' And Man stood aside from the struggle, resolving that God intended harmony to come out of chaos by human efforts. . . . And God smiled; and when he saw that Man had become perfect in renunciation and worship, he sent another sun through the sky, which crashed into Man's sun; and all returned again to nebula.

" 'Yes,' he murmured, 'it was a good play; I will have it performed again.' " *Why I Am Not a Christian* (New York: Simon & Schuster, 1967), pp. 105–6.

17. *Plague,* p. 205.

18. *Plague,* p. 198.

19. *Plague,* p. 205.

20. *Plague,* p. 206.

21. *Plague,* p. 203.

22. *Plague,* p. 211.

23. Martin Buber, *Eclipse of God* (New York: Harper & Brothers, 1952), pp. 117–19.

Notes to Chapter IV

1. It should be emphasized that the counterevidence approach advanced here refers to concrete experience—not an abstract idea or theoretical concoction. It is the complex of experiences packed into the category of ethnic suffering that stands as possible counterevidence against God's universal benevolence.

2. *God of Evil*, p. 72.

3. *God of Evil*, p. 72.

Notes to Chapter V

1. James Cone, *A Black Theology of Liberation* (New York: Lippincott, 1970), pp. 120–21.

2. *Liberation,* pp. 59–60.

3. *Liberation,* p. 115.

4. J. Deotis Roberts, *Liberation and Reconciliation: A Black Theology* (Philadelphia: Westminster Press, 1971), p. 83.

5. One point will establish that the multievidentiality of suffering is acknowledged by the black theologians, however inadvertently. Once the black theologian allows that deserved punishment is a possible interpretation of human suffering, and also denies that all suffering is deserved punishment, he cannot avoid the conclusion that suffering is multievidential.

6. *Liberation,* pp. 26–27.

7. *Liberation,* pp. 113–14.

Notes to Chapter VI

1. My criticism is directed solely against Washington's theology of suffering as presented in *The Politics of God*. Other parts of his thought, such as his view of the role of the black church as the *avant-garde* of black liberation, deserve the most sympathetic attention.

2. Consider, for example, *Stride Toward Freedom: The Montgomery Story* (New York: Harper & Brothers, 1958).

3. Joseph Washington, *The Politics of God* (Boston: Beacon Press, 1969), p. 155.

4. *Politics,* p. 155.

5. *Reconciliation,* p. 146.

6. *Politics,* p. 156.

7. *Politics,* p. 176.

8. *Politics,* p. 158.

9. Consider the discussion on pp. 99–100 of this book.

10. *Politics,* p. 163.

11. *Politics,* p. 155.

12. *Politics,* p. 171.

13. *Politics,* p. 156.

14. *Politics,* p. 159.

15. *Politics,* p. 166.

16. *Politics,* pp. 171–73.

17. *Politics*, p. 164.

18. I suggest that the more the black theologian is forced to respond to the issue of human or divine responsibility for the crimes of history the more attractive the position of humanocentric theism will become.

19. *Politics*, p. 160.

20. *Politics*, p. 159.

21. *Politics*, p. 157.

22. *Politics*, p. 157.

23. *Politics*, p. 148.

24. *Politics*, p. 148.

25. *Politics*, p. 160.

26. *Politics*, p. 166.

27. *Politics*, p. 159.

28. A basic assumption of non-violent resistance, according to Gandhi, is "the implicit belief that the sight of suffering on the part of multitudes of people will melt the heart of the aggressor and induce him to desist from his course of violence." John Somerville and Ronald Santoni, eds., *Social and Political Philosophy* (New York: Doubleday & Company, 1963), p. 539.

29. *Politics*, p. 172.

30. *Politics*, p. 170.

31. *Politics*, p. 157.

32. *Politics*, p. 157.

33. *Politics*, p. 173.

34. J. Deotis Roberts and James Gardiner, eds., *Quest for a Black Theology*, pp. 39–40.

35. *Liberation*, pp. 133–34.

Notes to Chapter VII

1. It has already been established that Cone advances the issue of divine racism as an inevitable question for black theology. Consequently it is not necessary to demonstrate this point.

2. *Liberation*, p. 241.

3. Cone defines "oppressed" in a way that departs radically from common usage. An essential feature of his definition is that the oppressed are the object of God's special concern and favor.

4. *Liberation*, pp. 108–9.

5. *Liberation*, p. 149.

6. *Liberation*, p. 181.

7. *Liberation*, p. 136.

8. *Liberation*, p. 132.

9. Several aspects of Cone's thought, as will be shown, necessitate the substantiation of the definitive event of liberation for blacks.

10. *Liberation*, pp. 25–26.

11. *Liberation*, p. 131.

12. *Liberation*, p. 100.

13. *Liberation*, p. 194.

14. *Liberation*, p. 100.

15. "Cone rejects the concept of eschatological compensation for this-worldly suffering, but, curiously, introduces something strikingly similar in content and intent: He finds it necessary to

postulate 'the future reality of life after death' for various reasons: to substantiate that God is on the side of blacks, to insure that fear of death will not lead to defeatism and thus diminish one's total commitment to the struggle, to assure that the death of the black freedom fighter is not meaningless, etc. One wonders, however, what the real difference is between the eschatological perspective he accepts and the one he rejects. The slave eschatology promised compensation for those who suffer patiently here, while Cone's eschatology guarantees reward and meaning for those who die valiantly here. Though the difference reflects a much-needed corrective for black ethics, is it an improvement on black theodicy? I raise this question because the following possibility sticks in my mind. Consider: the promise of a future reality after death motivates blacks to make the ultimate sacrifice for liberation, and this is the means by which a racist God beckons blacks to suicidal efforts and thus accomplishes black genocide." William Jones, "Theodicy and Methodology in Black Theology: A Critique of Washington, Cone and Cleage," *Harvard Theological Review*, 64:4 (October 1971), p. 553.

16. Emil Brunner, *The Christian Doctrine of Creation and Redemption* (Philadelphia: Westminster Press, 1952), p. 155.

17. *Liberation*, p. 149. Emphasis in the original.

18. *Liberation*, p. 248.

19. Consider also the following passage: "The future of God belongs to the future of the poor, the people who are assured that God's present righteousness will not be defeated by those who seek to usurp divine authority. The poor need not worry about the evil of this world; they will see the glory of Yahweh in their own fight against injustice." *Liberation*, pp. 243–44.

20. *Liberation*, p. 121.

21. *Liberation*, p. 66.

22. *Liberation*, pp. 19–20.

23. Note that the principle that God is the sum of his acts is affirmed here as well as in the next citation. Moreover, this principle is said to be a central biblical motif.

24. *Liberation*, p. 93.

25. *Liberation,* pp. 93–94.

26. *Liberation,* p. 91.

27. *Liberation,* p. 44.

28. *Liberation,* p. 149.

29. *Liberation,* p. 142.

30. *Liberation,* pp. 247–48.

31. *Liberation,* p. 133.

32. *Liberation,* p. 133.

33. *Liberation,* p. 21.

34. *Liberation,* pp. 131–32.

Notes to Chapter VIII

1. I would conclude that the most sympathetic and accurate framework for interpreting Cleage is that of a pragmatic theology. The crucial feature of this approach is its emphasis upon formulating arguments and categories that accomplish the specific goal at hand, rather than upon exhibiting a conscious concern to supply an accurate account of the nature of man, ultimate reality, etc. A pragmatic theology bypasses ontological description and validation.

Cleage's theological agenda appears to be that of weaning the black consciousness from its damnable attraction to whiteness and counterrevolutionary beliefs. His system is advanced as the quickest and most viable way of leading blacks to authentic blackness. This is accomplished primarily by simply transvaluing what blacks already accept as true. They believe in God, but a white God; so the pragmatic strategy here is to color God black.

If it is the case that we are dealing with a pragmatic theology, several consequences follow: We should not expect the theologian to tell us that this is in fact his approach. Indeed it is fatal to the pragmatic approach to reveal that it is present. Finally it is inappropriate to raise questions about the inner consistency or the "truth" value of its fundamental elements. The norm of a pragmatic theology is not truth but believability. The only appropriate question that can be addressed to it is, Does it work?

2. Cleage's latest work, *Black Christian Nationalism* (New York: William Morrow & Co., 1972) does not provide the necessary clarification, in my view.

3. Albert Cleage, *The Black Messiah* (New York: Sheed & Ward, 1969), p. 87.

4. "Because God has made the goal of black people his own

goal, Black Theology believes that it is not only appropriate but necessary to begin the doctrine of God with an insistence on his blackness. The blackness of God means that God has made the oppressed condition his own condition. . . . The blackness of God then means that the essence of the nature of God is to be found in the concept of liberation." *Liberation,* p. 121.

5. It is necessary to distinguish between Cleage's theory of a black God and that of Marcus Garvey, whom Cleage mentions. The following passage from Garvey does not attempt, as Cleage does, to affirm the one color of God to the exclusion of its opposite. Garvey insists only upon the right of each ethnic group to color God in its image. In this context the "real" color of God must always remain an open and unresolved question. This approach moves not toward a pigmentation theology but toward a theology of indigenization, which is a theology that starts from and expresses the particular perspective of a given ethnic community:

"If the white man has the idea of a white God, let him worship his God as he desires. If the yellow man's God is of his race, let him worship his God as he sees fit. We, as Negroes, have found a new ideal. Whilst our God has no color, yet it is human to see everything through one's own spectacles, and since the white people have seen their God through white spectacles, we have only now started . . . to see God through our own spectacles. . . . We Negroes believe in the God of Ethiopia, the everlasting God— God the Father, God the Son and God the Holy Ghost, the one God of all ages. That is the God in whom we believe, but we shall worship Him through the spectacles of Ethiopia." Marcus Garvey, *Philosophy and Opinions* (New York: Arno Press and N.Y. Times Co., 1969), p. 44.

6. "We know that Israel was a black nation, and that the descendants of the original black Jews are in Israel, Africa and the Mediterranean area today. The Bible was written by black Jews. The Old Testament is the history of black Jews. . . . Jesus was a black Messiah. He came to free a black people from the oppression of the white Gentiles. We know this to be a fact." *Messiah,* p. 111.

7. *Messiah,* pp. 53–54.

8. *Messiah,* p. 42.

9. *Messiah*, p. 43.

10. *Messiah*, p. 43.

11. The terms, for instance, are used interchangeably in the following statements: "Jesus was the non-white leader of a non-white people struggling for national liberation against the rule of a white nation." "Jesus was a revolutionary black leader, a Zealot, seeking to lead a Black nation to freedom." *Messiah,* pp. 3–4.

12. Quoted in Walter Kaufmann, *Nietzsche* (New York: Meridian Books, 1956), p. 47.

13. Numbers 14: 33.

14. *Messiah*, pp. 267–68.

15. *Messiah*, p. 271.

16. *Messiah*, p. 133.

17. *Messiah*, p. 242.

Notes to Chapter IX

1. Dietrich Bonhoeffer, *Letters and Papers from Prison,* ed. by Eberhard Bethge (London: Student Christian Movement Press, 1953), p. 124.

2. Major Jones, *Black Awareness; A Theology of Hope* (Nashville: Abingdon Press, 1971), p. 124.

3. In the discussion of humanocentric theism, Part III, I will indicate a basic similarity between this view and the concept of a God who acts in human history by means of "persuasion."

4. *Awareness,* p. 125.

5. *Awareness,* p. 133.

6. *Awareness,* p. 128.

7. *Awareness,* p. 128.

8. *Letters,* p. 17. Quoted in *Awareness,* p. 124.

9. *Awareness,* p. 125.

10. *Awareness,* p. 12.

11. *Awareness,* p. 16.

12. *Awareness,* p. 136.

13. *Awareness,* p. 129.

14. *Awareness,* p. 41.

15. *Awareness,* p. 13.

16. Geddes Hanson, "Black Theology and Protestant Thought," *Social Progress* (September–October 1969), p. 10. Quoted in *Awareness,* p. 14.

Notes to Chapter X

1. J. Deotis Roberts, "Black Consciousness in Theological Perspective," in *Quest for a Black Theology,* ed. by James Gardiner and J. Deotis Roberts (Philadelphia: The Pilgrim Press, 1971), p. 71.

2. *Consciousness*, p. 73.

3. "It is not surprising that longing for 'heaven' kept hope alive in 'souls of black folk.' Even if this was bad theology, it was good psychology. It was soothing like balm 'as it cheered the weary travellers along the heavenly road.'" *Reconciliation*, p. 172.

4. "The theme of the 'waiting God' is unacceptable for those who have been waiting so long and who are tired of waiting. This is bad psychology—even if it turns out to be good theology." *Consciousness*, p. 81.

5. *Negro's God*, pp. 71–72.

6. Mays describes a variant of this theme in the following passage: "It is the view of some that it is useless to call a doctor because when God gets ready for you all the doctors in the world cannot save you; if your time has not come, you will not die regardless of the seriousness of the case." *Negro's God*, p. 72.

7. Cf. Vincent Harding's "The Religion of Black Power," *The Religious Situation 1968,* ed. by Donald Cutler (Boston: Beacon Press, 1969).

8. *Reconciliation*, p. 99.

9. J. Deotis Roberts, "Black Theology and the Theological Revolution," *The Journal of Religious Thought,* 27 (Spring–Summer 1971), p. 14.

10. *Reconciliation,* p. 83.

11. *Reconciliation,* p. 96.

12. *Reconciliation,* p. 157.

13. *Theological Revolution,* p. 111.

14. *Consciousness,* p. 73.

15. *Consciousness,* p. 74.

16. *Reconciliation,* p. 96.

17. *Reconciliation,* p. 93.

18. *Reconciliation,* pp. 86–87.

19. *Reconciliation,* p. 90.

20. *Consciousness,* p. 74.

21. *Reconciliation,* p. 54.

22. Has Roberts forgotten his endorsement of Washington here?

23. *Reconciliation,* pp. 52–53.

24. *Reconciliation,* p. 59.

25. *Reconciliation,* p. 59.

26. *Consciousness,* p. 70.

27. *Reconciliation,* p. 156.

28. *Reconciliation,* p. 156.

29. *Consciousness,* p. 81.

30. *Reconciliation,* p. 157.

31. *Reconciliation,* p. 160.

32. *Reconciliation,* p. 146.

33. *Reconciliation,* p. 172.

34. *Reconciliation,* p. 143.

Notes to Chapter XI

1. This was the purpose of Part I of the study.

2. Though I do not regard the term "secular" to be an appropriate modifier, I employ it here because of its common usage. Secular humanism is often defined as the opposite of Christian humanism, and it is this essential difference I wish to emphasize.

3. This principle is apparently endorsed by each of the black theologians investigated, with the possible exception of Cone. In a dialogue with William Hordern he argues, "Because oppressors are the persons who devise the language tools for communication, their canons of logic do not include a form of discourse that is consistent with the liberation of the oppressed. . . . The oppressed . . . must deny the accepted canons of logic, allowing the liberation struggle *alone* to be the logical test for meaningful discourse. Logical consistency, as defined by the oppressors, is irrelevant." James Cone and William Hordern, "Dialogue on Black Theology," *Christian Century,* 88:37 (Sept. 15, 1971), p. 1079. It is not clear whether Cone intends to abandon the principle of internal consistency or the canon of non-contradiction. We must await a more detailed catalogue from Cone of the content of the oppressor's logical maxims.

4. Several of Rubenstein's insights have made an indelible impression upon my theological perspective. Every black theologian should wrestle with his conclusions. He dramatically illustrates an example of a prolegomenon that handles the critical task effectively but fails to accomplish the constructive objective.

5. *Auschwitz,* p. x.

6. Richard Rubenstein, "Homeland and Holocaust: Issues in

the Jewish Religious Situation," *The Religious Situation 1968,* ed. by Donald Cutler (Boston: Beacon Press, 1968).

7. *Auschwitz,* p. 46.

8. *Auschwitz,* p. 139.

9. *Homeland,* p. 56.

10. *Auschwitz,* p. 152.

11. *Auschwitz,* p. 198.

12. *Auschwitz,* p. 153.

13. *Auschwitz,* pp. 117–18.

14. Part IV, chapter I, section II.

15. Jean-Paul Sartre, *Anti-Semite and Jew,* trans. by George J. Becker (New York: Schocken Books, 1948), pp. 55–57.

16. *Auschwitz,* pp. 258–60.

Notes to Chapter XII

1. *God of Love,* p. 280.

2. I regard the principle of functional ultimacy to be the acknowledged norm of humanism and the unacknowledged standard for theism. The principle is another way of stating Protagoras' dictum, "Man is the measure of all things." I interpret this to mean that man can only act as if he were ultimate in the realm of values or history or both. It may well be the case that, ontologically speaking, he is not ultimate, but nonetheless it is necessary for him to choose, to valuate, regardless of the character of the rest of reality. This situation of man does not change, whether God exists or not. My own approach universalizes this principle and interprets it as the consequence of man's freedom.

Another way to explain the principle is in terms of what I would call the humanocentric predicament. It is impossible for man to shed his nature like a snake's skin and experience reality from another perspective. We should preface all our statements with the phrase, "in relation to man" or "in relation to man's measure." It is for this reason that I stress the functional, not the ontological, ultimacy of man. For man cannot obtain that lookout point where he can view man and determine if he is in reality the highest item. Sartre expresses the view intended here when he differentiates between types of humanism: "One may understand by humanism a theory which upholds man as the end-in-itself and as the supreme value. . . . This kind of humanism is absurd, for only the dog or horse would be in a position to pronounce a general judgment upon man and declare that he is magnificent." *Existentialism and Humanism,* trans. by Philip Mairet (London: Methuen & Co., 1948), p. 55.

3. Martin Buber, *Hasidism* (New York: Philosophical Library, 1948), pp. 108–9. Emphasis supplied.

4. *Hasidism,* pp. 67–68.

5. Harvey Cox, *The Secular City* (New York: The Macmillan Co., 1968), pp. 231–32.

6. *City,* p. 226.

7. *City,* pp. 20–21.

8. *City,* p. 31.

9. *City,* p. 229.

10. *City,* p. 227.

11. In a book that could be a paraphrase of the position of humanocentric theism, *You Shall Be as Gods,* Erich Fromm appears to enlarge the concept of human freedom so that it involves man's veto over God: "The very fact that man has made himself independent and does not need God any longer, the fact of having been defeated by man is precisely what pleases God. . . . 'It is a grace to God that His Zaddikim [the Hasidic masters] overrule him.'" Erich Fromm, *You Shall Be as Gods* (New York: Fawcett World Library, 1966), p. 64.

12. Howard Burkle, *The Non-Existence of God* (New York: Herder & Herder, 1969), pp. 201–2.

13. *Non-Existence,* p. 207.

14. *Non-Existence,* pp. 203–4.

15. Kierkegaard, *Journals,* no. 616.

16. There is no need for secular humanism to deny this claim, for it affirms the functional, not ontological, ultimacy of man. Its essential affirmation is the freedom of man, not the non-existence of God.

17. *Non-Existence,* pp. 214–16.

18. *Non-Existence,* p. 212.

19. *City,* p. 29.

20. *Reconciliation,* p. 156.

21. *God of Love,* p. 372.

22. *God of Love,* p. 397.

23. *God of Love,* p. 377.

24. *God of Love,* p. 398.

25. *Liberation,* p. 150.

26. *Awareness,* p. 127.

27. *Liberation,* p. 129.

28. *Liberation,* p. 125.

29. *Awareness,* p. 124.

INDEX

Abraham and Isaac, 59–60

Acts and action. *See also* Quietism; specific writers
God as the sum of His acts, 10–15
Mays and reciprocal dependence of belief and, 40–42

Adam and Eve, 15

Africans, and time, 14

After Auschwitz (Rubenstein), xvi, 177. *See also* Rubenstein, Richard

Alves, Rubem, Roberts' criticism of, 161

Anasahs, Aryans and, 3, 4

Anderson, Bernhard, quoted on Old Testament, 13

Anti-Semite and Jew (Sartre) 182–83

Arendt, Hannah, 182

Aryans, Anasahs and, 3, 4

Atheism
Burkle on theism and, 194
Cullen's works and, 28 ff., 33–35
and Sontag's apologia for theism, 64–65

Auschwitz, xvi, 87, 176 ff.
and Hick's theodicy, 198–200
Rubenstein's denial that suffering can be likened to Job's, 22

Baldwin, James, 37

Being and Nothingness (Sartre), 182

Belief, Mays and reciprocal dependence of action and, 40–42

Benevolence of God, xix, 7–9 ff., 33, 144. *See also* Theodicy
Mays and, 148
Roberts' (*see* Roberts, J. Deotis)
Washington and, 94

Bible (biblical sources), 142. *See also* New Testament; Old Testament; specific books
and God as sum of His acts, 13
plague in, 47
view of suffering, 15–20, 23

Black Christ, The (Cullen), 28–34

"Black Man's God, The" (Roberts), 73

Black Messiah, The (Cleage), 121–31

Blackness of God, Cleage and, 122–26

Bonhoeffer, Dietrich, Major Jones and, 133, 134, 136, 200

Bowker, John, quoted on religion and suffering, 21, 206

Brunner, Emil, Cone and, 105–6, 108

Buber, Martin, 187–89 ff.
  and Kierkegaard's "teleological
    suspension of the ethical,"
    59
Burkle, Howard, 191–94

Calvary. See also Cross, the
  and salvation, 7–8
Camus, Albert, xv, 42–57, 181,
    183
  and conversion, 67
  and multievidentiality of suffer-
    ing, 7–9
Cannibal Mother Earth, 179, 180
Chosen people (the elect), 75–76.
    See also Suffering servant
  Cleage and, 127 ff.
  Cone and, 99 ff.
  Jews as. See Jews
  Joseph Washington and, 80 ff.,
    84 ff., 94
Christ. See Jesus Christ
Cleage, Albert, 101, 117, 121–31
Color (Cullen), 26–27
Cone, James, xv, 9, 72–73, 75,
    76–77, 96–97, 98–120, 200,
    201
Conversion, gnosiological, 67–68
Cox, Harvey, 189–91, 194
Cross, the, 7, 19, 22
  Roberts and, 81, 162 ff.
Crucifixion, the, 7–8. See also
  Cross, the
Cullen, Countee, 26–35

Death, 21–22
  Cone on immortality, 170
  Rubenstein on, 179
Death-of-God theology, 176
Demonic God, xvi, 6 ff., 51–52

Bertrand Russell's portrayal of,
  39
Joseph Washington and, 90
De novo theology, 76–78. See also
  specific writers
Deserved punishment. See Punish-
  ment
Deuteronomic theory, suffering
  servant contrasted with, 16
Du Bois, W. E. B., xviii

Egypt, ancient, 93, 113. See also
  Exodus
Election. See Chosen people
Eschatology (eschaton), 11 ff.,
    20, 36, 131, 174–75
  Camus and, 46, 49 ff.
  Cone and, 105, 114 ff.
  Jones and, 136–39
  Metz and, xvii
  Roberts and, 156, 158, 160–66
  Washington's theories and, 81,
    88, 90
Ethics, and ethical nihilism, 63
Ethnic suffering, xvii, 20–23, 29,
    36, 74 ff., 151 ff., 174 ff. See
    also Oppression; specific
    writers
  humanocentric theism and,
    185–202
Exaltation (exaltation event), 18–
    19, 20, 22, 28. See also Lib-
    eration
  Cone and, 100, 113
  Roberts and, 158
  Washington's theories and, 80–
    81 ff., 88, 90
Exodus, 18
  Cleage and, 123

Exodus (*cont'd*)
Cone and, 113, 114, 116–17, 118
Cox and, 190
Roberts and, 162

Forster, Bernhard, quoted on bright figure of Savior, 126
Freedom, 10–11, 87, 89, 191 ff. *See also* Liberation; Oppression
Fromm, Erich, quote from *You Shall Be as Gods,* 230

Galatians, and I-You relationship between God and man, 189
Gandhi, Mohandas K., Joseph Washington and views of, 89
Garvey, Marcus, and color of God, 222
Genesis
Abraham and Isaac story, 59–60
and sin and suffering, 58
Gnosiological conversion, 67–68
God, Why Did You Do That? (Sontag), xvi
God of Evil, The (Sontag), xvi
Golgotha, 7–8, 50, 64
Gospels, the, 43. *See also* specific books
Gossett, Thomas, and *Rig Veda,* 3
Gruber, Heinrich, Rubenstein on, 178

Hanson, Geddes, Major Jones cites, 142–43

Harding, Vincent, Preface to *The Negro's God* by, 25–26
Helpless God, Jones and, 134–35, 200
Hick, John, 197–200
and function of theodicy, 185
quoted on suffering, 50, 198–99
Hindu scriptures (*Rig Veda*), 3, 4
Hitler, Adolf, 106
Hick and, 200
Rubenstein's view of, 92, 106, 178
Hope, theologies of, 149, 197–200
Hordern, William, 227
"How Black Is Black Religion?" (Washington), 94
Humanism, xv, 46, 53, 139. *See also* Secular humanism
Humanistic theism, 172, 176, 185–202
black theology, theological reconstruction, and, 200–2
essentials of, 186–94
Hick's theodicy, 197–200
theodicy of, 194–96

Immanence of God, Cone and, 115
Immortality, Cone on, 107
Indra (Hindu God), 3, 4
Isaac, Abraham and, 59–60
Isaiah, suffering-servant theme and liberation in, xviii, 18, 20
Israelites. *See* Jews

Jeremiah, question on suffering, 19

Jesus Christ, 7–8, 19, 50. *See also*
    Cross, the; Resurrection
    Cleage and, 122, 123, 126
    Cone and, 100, 111, 112, 117,
        118
    Cox and, 189, 190
    Cullen works on, 28–35
    Jones and, 133
    Luke (biblical) on, 58
    Peter (biblical) on, 16
    Roberts and, 158
Jews (Israelites), xvi, 21, 175–84.
    See also Exodus; Ruben-
    stein, Richard
    Cleage on, 122, 123, 126 ff.
    Cone on, 100, 112 ff.
    Roberts and, 158
    Washington on, 81–82, 84, 86,
        88, 92–93, 94
Job, 19
    Roberts and, 156, 157
    Rubenstein denies suffering of
        Jews can be likened to test-
        ing of, 22
Jones, Major, 101, 132–44, 200 ff.

Kierkegaard, Søren, 192–93, 212
    Buber and, 59
    Camus and, 46, 51
King, Martin L., and suffering,
    80, 89, 96
Kingdom (of God), 58, 89
    Cone and, 112
    Rubenstein and, 183

Larsen, Nella, 38–39
"Leap of faith," 46, 52–53
Liberation, 9, 18 ff., 22, 28, 41,
    68, 72 ff., 172, 173. *See also*
    Eschatology; Oppression

Cleage and, 121, 123
Cone   and,   76–77,   98 ff.,
    106 ff., 111–20
Jones and, 137, 139–44
Roberts and, 145–66
Washington and, 80 ff., 88 ff.,
    95
Love, 7, 11, 201. *See also* Benev-
    olence of God
    Cone and God's, 102
Luke, Book of, 58

Macquarrie, John, quoted on om-
    nipotence, 200
Marx, Karl, and religion as opi-
    ate, 43
Marxist theism, 194
Matthew, Book of, and Christ as
    cosufferer, 133
Mays, Benjamin, 25–26, 147–48
    and belief and action, 40–41
    and black humanism, xv
Messiah, Rubenstein and the, 179
Metz, Johannes, and eschatology,
    xvii
Moloch, 60
Moltmann, Jürgen, 197, 198
    quoted on theodicy, xx

*Negro's God as Reflected in His
    Literature, The* (Mays), 25–
    26, 40–41, 147–48
New Age, the, 58
Newby, I. A., and "religious rac-
    ism," 3
New Testament. *See also* specific
    parts
    Cleage on, 101
    Cone on, 112, 117–18
    on suffering, 16

New York, end of slavery in, 210

Noah, 15

Non-violence, 217. *See also* Vicarious suffering

Nygren, Anders, and Calvary, 7

Old Testament, 13, 189. *See also* Bible; specific parts
Bowker on suffering in, 21

Omnipotence, God's. *See* Theodicy; specific writers

Oppression, 73, 126, 138, 143–44, 175, 201, 202. *See also* Liberation; Punishment; Suffering
Cone and, 98–120
Jewish. *See* Jews; Rubenstein, Richard
theodicy, quietism, and, 40–60

"Pagan Prayer" (Cullen), 28, 34

Paul, Nathaniel, 35–36

Payne, Buchner, 4–5

Payne, Daniel A., 35, 36

Persuasion, Burkle and divine, 192 ff.

Peter, first letter of, 16

Plague, The (Camus), 42–57

Plato, and belief and action, 40

Politics of God, 75–76

Politics of God, The (Washington), 79, 94, 95, 200. *See also* Washington, Joseph

Poverty, Martin L. King and, 96

Prolegomenon, nature of a, 169–72

Providence, 115

Psychology of hope, Jones and, 139–41

Psychology of liberation, Roberts and, 145–66

Punishment, 15, 18, 95, 173
Camus's *The Plague* and, 47 ff., 55 ff.
Cleage and, 121, 126–31
Cone and, 102, 103–5, 116
Jones and, 136
Roberts and, 154 ff.
Washington and, 81, 83

Quicksand (Larsen), 38–39

Quietism, 40–60, 96
Cleage and, 127, 128
Cone and, 105
humanocentric theism and, 195–97
Mays and, 148

Rebel, The (Camus), 42, 49–50

Reconciliation, 173; Roberts and, 145, 150

Redemptive suffering. *See* Punishment; Suffering servant; specific writers

Resurrection, the, 19, 23, 50
Cone's theories and, 111, 117–19
Roberts' theories and, 81, 162 ff.

Revelation, Cone and, 112 ff.

Rig Veda, Gossett's interpretation of, 3, 4

Roberts, J. Deotis, 9, 81, 141, 144, 145–66, 200
"Black Man's God" quoted, 73
Cone and, 101, 102
and Moltmann, 198

Rubenstein, Richard, xvi, 87, 92, 175–84

Rubenstein, Richard (*cont'd*)
   and Cone, 106
   denies Auschwitz can be lik-
     ened to testing of Job, 22
   and Hitler, 92, 106, 178
Russell, Bertrand, 212
   and demonic God, 39

Salvation, xviii–xix, 5, 7, 8, 17,
   18, 90 ff., 102, 103. *See also*
   Punishment;   Resurrection,
   the; Suffering
Sartre, Jean-Paul, xv, 67, 181–83
Secular City, The (Cox), 189–91
Secular humanism, 171, 172, 176,
   180 ff., 186, 194
Sexism, black theologians and,
   126
Sexuality of God, combination
   methodology and, 125
Sin, 15 ff., 57, 104, 105, 127 ff.
   See also Punishment; Suffer-
   ing; specific writers
Sinai Covenant, Cox's concept of,
   190
Sisyphus, 196
Slavery
   abolition in New York, 210
   Mays and, 148
   and survival, 150
   Washington and, 91, 92
Sodom, 15
Sontag, Frederick, xvi, 64–65
Sovereignty of God. *See* Theod-
   icy; specific writers
Suffering, xvii ff., 11 ff. *See also*
   Ethnic suffering; Oppres-

sion; Punishment; Vicarious
   suffering; specific writers
   multievidentiality of, 6–9, 74
   radical interpretation of black,
     24–26. *See also* specific writ-
     ers
   toward a biblical view of, 15–
     20
Suffering servant, 16–20, 113,
   127, 157–58. *See also* Exaltation; Vicarious suffering;
   specific writers
   Washington and, 79–97, 110
Survival, 149–50

Theism, 53, 149. *See also* Atheism; specific writers
   apologia of Sontag, 64–65
   humanistic, 172, 176, 185–202
   theocentric, 187, 201
Theocentric theism, 187, 201
Theodicy, xv–xvi ff., 33, 205. *See*
   also specific writers
   Camus's critique of, 45–47.
     See also Camus, Albert
   demonstrative, 47–48
   essentials of viable black, 173–
     76
   and humanocentric theism,
     194–97
   of last resort, 48–53
   oppression, quietism, and, 40–
     60
   prop for oppression, 42–45
"Theodicy for Today, A" (Hick),
   197
Time, African concept of, 14
Transcendence, Cone's theories
   and divine, 108–9

Vicarious suffering, 79–80, 99–
    103, 136. *See also* Suffering
    servant; specific writers

Washington, Booker T., glorifica-
    tion by whites, 24
Washington, Joseph, 9, 79–97,
    200
  and Cone's theodicy, 110
  Roberts and, 157–58

Woodson, Carter G., 37–38
Wrath, God's. *See also* Punish-
    ment
  Cone and, 102, 103
  Jones and, 135–36

Yette, Samuel, 9
You Shall Be as Gods (Fromm),
    230